A
SIKH
FAMILY
IN
BRITAIN

D1743374

MAN AND RELIGION SERIES
Part I
Families and Faiths

RELIGIOUS EDUCATION PRESS
A Division of Pergamon Press

A SIKH
FAMILY
IN BRITAIN

W. Owen Cole

ACKNOWLEDGEMENTS

The author wishes to thank the following for their help in the production of this book:

The High Commissioner of India.
The Pakistan Embassy
The Times Newspaper.
Mr. Piara Singh Sambhi upon whose friendship, advice and guidance he has relied heavily and to whom he wishes to express particular gratitude.
The Sikh Community of Leeds without whose kindness and co-operation this book could not have been written.
"Telegraph and Argus" for the photograph at the opening of Guru Gobind Singh Gurdwara, Bradford, March 1972.
Ram Studio and Camera Dealers of Southall for the photograph of the opening of the Punjabi School at Southall.

W. Owen Cole
is
Senior Lecturer in Religious Studies West Sussex Institute of Higher Education, Chichester

Illustrations
Brigitt Head

MAN AND RELIGION SERIES
General Editor   Ronald Dingwall
Art Director   Keith Clements

RELIGIOUS EDUCATION PRESS
A Division of Pergamon Press
Hennock Road, Exeter EX2 8RP

First published 1973
Reprinted 1973, 1975, 1978, 1982

Made and printed in Great Britain by
A. Wheaton & Co. Ltd.,
Exeter

Library of Congress Catalog Card No.
77-175199
ISBN 0 08 016525 7 non net
ISBN 0 08 017631 3 net

IN THIS BOOK

DEDICATION

To my daughters Eluned and Sian, to their
schoolfriends Gulsharn and Tajvir and to
Jaswant who was born while this book was
being written—in the hope that they may grow
to adulthood in a Britain that is at one with itself.

FOREWORD On the cover of this book is the sacred emblem of the Sikhs. It is to be seen on their flags; some Sikhs wear it in the turban or on the lapel of their jackets. You may also see it as a design on a tie worn by a Sikh. It is called the **Khanda.**

There are three parts to the emblem. First the two-edged sword, pointing upwards, then the circle and finally the two cutting swords.

The two-edged sword is also called **Khanda.** With such a sword Guru Gobind Singh stirred the **amrit** when he created the **Khalsa**, the Sikh brotherhood of soldier-saints. These men were to be two-edged, not merely soldiers but also men of God: fighters, but only in the cause of Truth. The **Khanda** is the sword of true knowledge which drives away ignorance and superstition.

Outside Coventry Cathedral is a sculpture by Sir Jacob Epstein showing St. Michael defeating the Devil. Another popular Christian idea is that of St. George slaying the Dragon. Sikhs have a similar belief in the defeat of evil. Guru Gobind Singh composed a Hymn of the Sword in which he described God as a sword, the Destroyer of the armies of the Wicked.

The two cutting swords are called **kirpans.** They are the weapons of men who defend the cause of truth, not in the dark with an assassin's dagger, but in the open. Guru Arjan, first martyr of the Sikhs, instructed his young son to sit on the throne armed. The two swords represent his spiritual power as guru of the Sikhs and his temporal power as their ruler.

The circle or **chakra** has many meanings for Indians. For the Sikhs, besides other things, it is a reminder that God is one, without beginning or end, that the **Khalsa** is one, and that all men are brothers. The **kara** or bracelet which a Sikh wears on his right wrist reminds him of the same ideas.

Khalsa, kara, kirpan and a number of other words I have mentioned will be completely unknown to you, just as the Sikhs may be strangers to you. Mr. Cole has written this book to help you to understand our beliefs and our way of life and it gives me great pleasure to write the foreword to it.

I hope that when you have read *A Sikh Family in Britain* you will want to meet us. I am sure I speak for all Sikhs when I say you will be welcome visitors to one of our **Gurdwaras.**

Meanwhile, I hope you will enjoy reading about us.

Best wishes and greetings from me and from all Sikhs.

Piara Singh Sambhi
President of the Sikh Temple, Leeds 1967-1970
and founder member of the Central Committee
of British Sikhs.

INTRODUCTION Kishan and Alan are both 16-year-old boys preparing to take 'O' levels next summer. They are in the same groups for Geography, English and a few other subjects, so they know one another fairly well. They travel home on the same bus and one day while they were waiting at the stop Alan turned to his friend and asked him a question.

"Kishan, last Tuesday when Mr. Clegg was talking about India he said that we ought to find

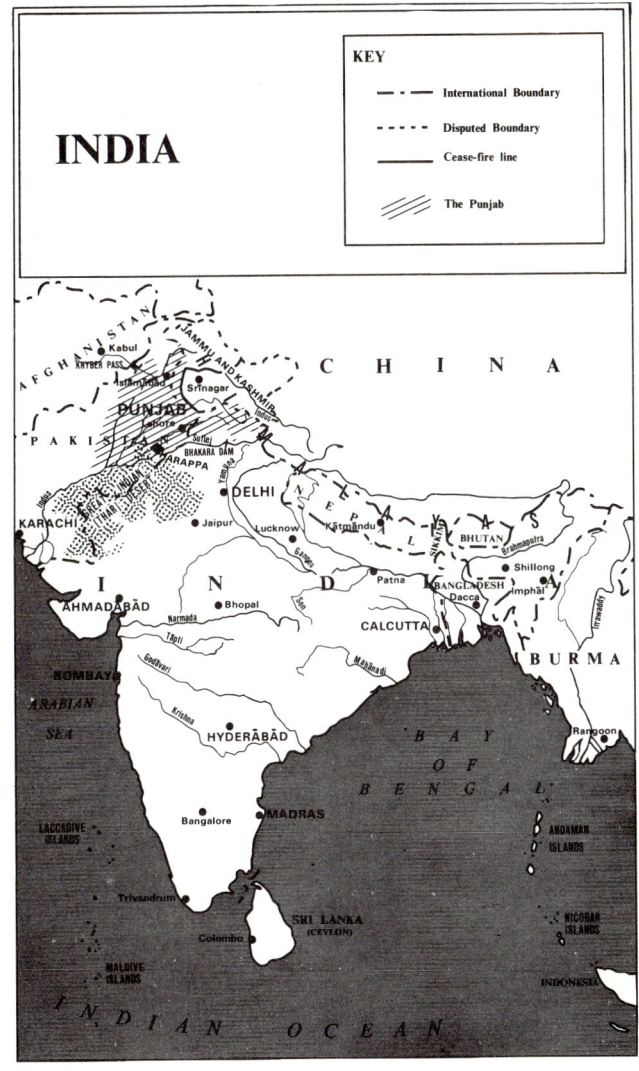

out things about its many religions. Besides Hindus mainly in India and Moslems mainly in Pakistan, he said there were some Buddhists and some Christians and also Sikhs. He said you were a Sikh. I thought Sikhs were a sort of soldier with turbans and black beards and called Singh. My dad was a soldier during the war and he told me about Sikhs. But you're not a soldier, your name is Ruprai, not Singh, and you certainly haven't a beard!"

Kishan laughed, "I'm afraid you English don't bother to find out very much about your neighbours. In 1849 we became part of British India and you ruled us for nearly 100 years but even now, when some of us live in England, we are still strangers to you."

"I suppose that's true", said Alan. "But Mr. Clegg said you have a religion of your own. Have you? Where is your church? Do you believe in God? Why did you come to England? Who are the Sikhs, anyway?"

"Wait a minute", said Kishan. "I can't answer all those questions at once. It will take weeks—but if you really want to know I can tell you some things when we are travelling on the bus and you can come to my home and one Sunday you might like to come with me to what you call church.

"Your last question is an easy one, Alan. I was born in Britain—here in Leeds. I still live in the house where I was born. As for the rest, it will take more than a few minutes to answer them."

1   WHO ARE THE SIKHS?

This was Alan's sixty-four-thousand dollar question.

There are many answers.

Many Britons who fought in the Second World War would say that they were the finest soldiers in the Indian army.

Travellers might describe them as taxi-drivers, engine-drivers or engineers, distinguished by their turbans, found in Hong Kong, Singapore, many large cities of East Africa, as well as in Bombay, Delhi and Calcutta.

A Hindu would probably tell you that they were a religious minority of between seven and ten million people living in the Punjab and following the teachings of Nanak, an Indian who was born five hundred years ago.

All these statements are correct and put together they provide the answer to Alan's question.

The Sikhs number less than one fiftieth of the population of India which probably reached 500 millions in 1967. They have their own religion and it is one of the world's most recent. '**Sikh**' comes from a **Sanskrit** word meaning 'disciple'. Sikhs follow the teachings of Guru Nanak who was born in *C.E. 1463 (**Guru** means teacher). Nanak disliked violence and war; he worked to establish peace between Hindu and Moslem. His followers were often persecuted and eventually, after almost two hundred years, decided that it was right to defend

---

* Since the terms B.C. (Before Christ) and A.D. (Anno Domini, In the year of our Lord) have a specifically Christian significance, it is now usual in books on World Religions to use the expressions B.C.E. (Before the Common Era) and C.E. (In the Common Era). Sometimes books written in India give Bikram (Vikram) year dates, 1972 being S. (Samrat) 1915. Guru Nanak was born in 1469 C.E., that is S. 1526.

liberty with the sword. Sikhs have always been travellers. They are found throughout the East, in Africa and in Canada as well as Britain, working as farmers and engineers, teachers and doctors.

The purpose of this book is to help you to know about these people, to tell you of their ideas, way of life and history so that when you meet them you will not have the odd ideas that Alan had in the beginning. But the Sikhs are people and the only way to get to know people is by meeting them, getting to know them and becoming friends.

2   WHY DID THE SIKHS COME TO BRITAIN?

Man is a migrant. He always has been. He always will be. Plans are already being made to colonise the moon. By C.E. 2000 the manned exploration of other planets in the solar system will have begun and pioneers will be switching their attention to the galaxies and planetary systems which lie farther away.

But let us come back to earth. To Britain. Which of us can claim to be the true British? Perhaps the Welsh or the Irish.

Our island has been a melting pot of races for as long as historians can remember. Here is a list of people who have settled in Britain since 400 C.E.

Angles and Saxons—from Germany
Jutes—perhaps from the Rhineland
Vikings and Danes—from Scandinavia
Normans
Flemings
Huguenots
Jews
Irish
Poles
Italians
Hungarians

These people came for a number of reasons, some to find freedom from persecution—the Jews, Huguenots and Hungarians—some because there was not enough land for them back home—Angles, Saxons, Jutes and possibly Vikings—and others to better themselves economically—the Irish especially.

Meanwhile let us remember that these same reasons sent Scots to Canada and New Zealand, Welsh to Patagonia, Roman Catholics to Maryland and Quakers to Pennsylvania in America, English to Australia and South Africa.

Man has always been on the move and Britain has always been like an international air terminal with people coming and going.

Since the mid nineteen-fifties the people of Britain living in large cities such as London, Leeds and Birmingham, Bradford and Wolverhampton have noticed a steadily increasing number of West Indian and Asian people living in their communities. There are now about one million, most of them in Greater London, West Midlands, South East Lancashire, Merseyside, West Yorkshire and Tyneside. These are not students or sailors staying for a while but families buying houses and settling down, joining political parties and trade unions and becoming full members of the community. They will retain their religious beliefs and many of their customs and often continue to speak their native language at home. Even this is changing; there are 'Pakistanis' who were born in London and have as good a cockney accent as anyone else, and there are many 'Asians' and West Indians now eligible to play for Yorkshire at cricket because they were born in Yorkshire. They are already representing their schools and towns in a number of sports. But why are Asians and West Indians coming to Britain?

There are two answers to this question. One is historical, the other is economic.

Both these areas were part of the British Empire. The English language was learned in schools and English textbooks often used in the teaching of reading—books like 'Janet and John'. Stories about kings and queens of England formed part of the history syllabus. Shakespeare and Wordsworth were studied in literature lessons. England was the motherland.

They have also come for generations to receive a good education. Wealthy parents sent their sons

WHY DID THE SIKHS COME TO BRITAIN?

to Oxford or Cambridge from India fifty years ago. Others won scholarships enabling them to come.

Today everyone wants education. The world does not need unskilled labour, and people in Indian villages know that hopes of a good job depend on schooling; but in India and the Caribbean there are not enough schools, and certainly not enough places in secondary schools, for all who are competing for them. Parents have often saved very hard to send a child to a relative in Britain so that he can go to a good comprehensive school to work for his 'O' levels.

The main reason for immigration is economic. For those who want to leave the family small-holding in a village in India or Pakistan there is not much chance of work in the town. If a man finds work, wages in the West Indies or India are very low. At present rates a man might work for twenty years in those countries and still earn less than he would get in the lowest paid job in Britain in one year. The story goes that Dick Whittington was told that the streets of London were paved with gold, so he decided to leave home and seek his fortune there. People from Jullundur and Kingston, Gujurat and Kashmir are coming to Britain for the same reason today.

There are always hard jobs and dirty jobs which are poorly paid and which none of us wants to do. Irish 'navvies' have always been prepared to live in shacks or nowadays in caravans, and build our railways and motorways. Irish women have come to work in our hospitals. With full employment after the war London Transport, British Rail and some textile mills in the north could not find sufficient native employees. Asian and Caribbean immigrants came and did these jobs. After all, they could earn about £15 a week in some of them, as against £30 **a year** in Pakistan. Since 1962 controls of

Commonwealth immigration to Britain have
reduced the number entering the country and in
recent years most of those who have come have
been dependants of those already here, wives or
children, and teachers, doctors, engineers and
scientists. The world has too few of these, their
own countries cannot spare them, but Britain pays
them far more than their own countries can.

Perhaps we can best understand why Sikhs
came to Britain if we listen in to what Mr.
Ruprai told Alan and Kishan one day as he
gave them a lift home from school.

It was a dark miserable afternoon, the rain was
turning to snow and there was a strong wind.

Alan couldn't help thinking that there were
better places to live than England and said so.
He added "I don't know why you left the sunny,
hot Punjab, for this cold place, Mr. Ruprai.
You didn't have to, did you?"

"No", he said, "no one forced me to leave India
and I could return tomorrow, but perhaps one
day you will discover that there is more to
happiness than a sunny climate!"

"Why did you come?" said Kishan, "I've often
wanted to know".

"It is a long story", said his father, "and it
doesn't begin with me. Sikhs have always been
travellers. There have been no caste restrictions
to prevent them. Traditionally, as you know, Hindu
can only do the work which is fitting to their
particular caste, and many consider it wrong to lea
India for another country. We don't share
these beliefs, so for a hundred years Sikhs
were members of the British army, seeing the
world. They were taxi-drivers in Bombay,
policemen in Hong Kong and farmers in
Canada. Many would leave the Punjab for two
or three years, find work with good pay

abroad, send money home each month and eventually return. It was a way of earning money to buy more land or better tools, and build finer houses. In the Punjab there were often too many people and not enough jobs. It didn't need everyone in the family to run a small farm.

"It was the Second World War which really caused many Sikhs to think of emigrating. They came to Europe or to America or Australia and New Zealand in the army or air force and discovered the affluent society. Most people seemed to live in comfortable homes with electricity in them. Some had cars—though of course during the war they had no petrol to run them! Everyone they met could read and write and work was well paid. The memory of what they had seen remained in the minds of the ex-soldiers and they told their families about it.

"My eldest brother was one of the soldiers who never settled down in the Punjab. He was a good farmer but he decided to seek his fortune in England. He became a market trader and now has a shop. His family helped him raise enough money for his fare; after a year he was able to repay them and less than a year later he could afford to send for his wife and son.

"At that time I was still at school and doing quite well. I passed my examinations and thought I would like to work in the civil service or a bank, but there were not many opportunities. My brother said I would soon find work in England and he would look after me so I left the Punjab too. For a time I helped my brother and then began my own business. It prospered, I began making friends and decided England would be my new home. After three years I paid a visit to the Punjab where my family had arranged a marriage for me and when I came back to England Mrs. Ruprai came with me! We lived in a small flat, my wife found work and I was able to train to be an accountant.

"As you know, the population of India is very large, pay is very low compared with Britain—even if you can find work. A bus driver will earn about £10 per month, a teacher starts at about £20 per month. It is not surprising that a cousin of mine Dalip Singh who had a degree and worked in the civil service decided to come to Britain to work in a factory for three times his Indian salary, is it? Dalip came to Bradford where there was plenty of work but the factory owners were unable to find sufficient English labour. Soon he was writing to his friends back home telling them how well paid he was and assuring them of jobs where he was working if they cared to come. Many came, some brought their families, most came alone and later sent for their wives and children and sometimes parents to join them.

"Sometimes, Alan," said Mr. Ruprai, "we are criticised for taking the jobs and houses of the English people. This is not true. We have usually settled in cities where there were more jobs than people to fill them, we came in good years when there was little unemployment and plenty of over-time for everyone, and we have often bought and improved old houses which English people were leaving for better ones."

"I know", replied Alan, 'but my father says people don't seem as tolerant as they were a few years ago. Haven't any Sikhs thought of going back to India?'

"Yes, they have. Some who emigrate are always homesick. I've read of Britons emigrating to Australia and returning after three months. Some Sikhs didn't stay here long. Others are worried about the future and are saving money or buying plots of land at Chandigarh, Ludhiana or Delhi so that one day they can go home."

WHY DID THE SIKHS COME TO BRITAIN?

"Will you stay?" asked Alan.

"I will", Mr. Ruprai said without hesitation. "I will for a number of reasons. It would be difficult for me to set myself up in business in India or to join a partnership. After all, I've been away for 20 years, almost. My parents are dead and most of my relatives and my wife's are now here in England—in London, or Birmingham, Leeds or Bradford.

"If we went home Kishan and Pritam would have problems—neither speaks Punjabi well enough to get a job, and they scarcely read it at all. They would have to learn Punjabi or Hindi.

"Also Pritam has an Englishman's idea of India. She thinks it is full of snakes and she dislikes snakes. She thinks she would have to carry water from a well in a large jar on her head! One day I must take her back for a holiday so that she can discover the truth about India but she is too English to begin life there now!

"You see, Alan, Kishan and Pritam may be Sikhs and I hope they will grow up to be faithful ones, but they are also English. They will marry English Sikhs, it would be unfair to arrange a marriage for them with Sikhs from the Punjab who would be strangers here. One day, I expect, I shall be a grandfather. What pleasure is there in that if I am thousands of miles away in India? We shall not go back to India, our children and grandchildren will keep us here!

"Sometimes the English think we are very old-fashioned and domineering in the way we treat our children. Perhaps we are! If so it is only because we love them and feel that having brought them into the world we have the responsibility of helping them to avoid mistakes and benefit from our experience.

"Here's your home, Alan. Goodbye."

Alan had enjoyed his conversation with Mr.

Ruprai. He now felt he knew a little more about Kishan and his family, and the reasons which had brought them to Britain. But he also realised how little he really knew about that part of India from which Mr. Ruprai and his wife had come—the Punjab. He decided he would find out more about it, and so went to his local library to see what he could discover for himself. The next chapter tells you what he discovered.

ARRIVALS AND DEPARTURES: BRITAIN 1968, 1969, 1970 AND 1971

The total number of immigrants entering Britain in 1968 was 500,665. In 1969 there were 561,957. In 1970 there were 646,259. In 1971 there were 691,285.

Emigrants numbered 462,167 in 1968; 542,586 in 1969; 639,052 in 1970; 721,253 in 1971. The main sources of immigration and emigration were:

	1968		1969		1970		1971	
	Admitted	Embarked	Admitted	Embarked	Admitted	Embarked	Admitted	Embarked
Australia	82,391	86,836	89,815	92,392	106,866	116,739	118,413	138,100
Canada	166,875	186,753	211,132	229,151	244,054	260,956	269,109	305,295
Cyprus	10,594	8,650	10,677	11,166	10,043	10,615	9,935	11,580
India	65,665	37,325	59,319	46,981	65,815	57,399	72,892	66,303
Jamaica	16,057	14,681	16,241	17,603	18,544	19,815	20,429	22,796
New Zealand	20,973	24,725	21,755	25,153	26,371	31,303	27,399	34,899
Pakistan	39,166	24,290	40,729	27,917	43,139	33,251	37,644	32,001

From no other countries except Hongkong in 1971, Malaysia in 1970 and 1971, Malta in 1969, 1970 and 1971, and Nigeria in 1970 and 1971 did the annual total exceed 10,000. As there is no control over travel from Ireland, no statistics are available but it is thought that more immigrants come from Ireland than any other country.

It may come as a surprise to you to know that most immigrants come from Canada and Australia, but we generally read about those coming from India, Pakistan and East Africa. It is equally surprising to note that more people left for India than for New Zealand in each of these years.

Sikh immigrants are included in the figures for India; it is impossible to discover their precise numbers.

(The figures on this page were obtained from **Whitaker's Almanack** for 1970–1973. The last edition was published too early to take account of the large number of Asians with British passports who have been allowed into Britain after being expelled from Uganda.)

WHY DID THE SIKHS COME TO BRITAIN?   10

3

THE PUNJAB: THE HOME OF THE SIKHS

To avoid confusion it is important to realise that when the Punjab is mentioned in books it may mean a political area or it may describe a geographical region. If you are talking to a Moslem he will probably be thinking of the province of Pakistan which has Lahore as its capital. A Sikh will mean the the province in the Republic of India which has Chandigarh as its administrative centre. The writer of a geography book may not be very concerned about boundaries between countries. He includes both provinces in his description of the Punjab.

THE PUNJAB IS A GEOGRAPHICAL EXPRESSION

The Indian subcontinent is roughly the size of Europe without Russia. It has a rich variety of races, languages and religions, and the term Hinduism which is usually used of the main religion of the subcontinent covers a greater range of ideas and practices than does the word Christianity in Europe.

Geographically India may be divided into four main zones:

1. The high mountain ranges running from sea to to sea and defining the natural frontiers.
2. The plain of the Ganges which many Indians recognise as the real Hindustan.
3. South of the Narbada river the uplands of the Indian peninsula, the Deccan.
4. The valley and plain of the Indus. The lower part is called Sind, the upper the Punjab.

Punjab means 'five streams'. These are the rivers Jhelum, Chenab, Ravi, Beas and Sutlej which rise in the Himalayas and flow into the river Indus. It has an area of some 55,000 square miles. On the northern edge are foothills which quickly become the mountains of the Himalayas. To the

PUNJAB TODAY

KEY
- · — · — International Boundary
- · · · · Disputed Boundary
- ——— Cease-fire line
- Punjab Province
- The Punjab

south and east is the Thar desert and to the west
are the mountains of the north-west frontier.

The main feature of the Punjab is the plain
through which the five rivers wind before coming
together and then joining the Indus. Such a plain,
so well watered, should be fertile. It is, but life is
a constant struggle between the sun and wind,
which attempt to take the water from the land, and
man who seeks to retain and use it.

THE PUNJAB—HOME OF THE SIKHS

The average temperatures for early spring and late autumn are over 21°C and in summer these exceed 35°C and often reach 45°C.

The area between each of the rivers is called the **doab**, 'two waters', and these are intensely cultivated but depend for water supply upon irrigation in the form of canals carrying water from the rivers, or deep wells. Two-thirds of the land under cultivation relies on irrigation.

Farmers in the Punjab are more fortunate than many in India. By March the rivers are carrying water provided by the melting Himalayan snows but by July, when the monsoons begin, the rivers are almost dry again. In fact, were it not for irrigation water seeping back into the river beds these would probably dry up by June.

The monsoons bring about fifteen inches of rain in three months, but by October they have come to an end and until the cycle begins again in March farmers depend on the water they have been able to trap.

In winter, night frosts are common and in summer there are dust storms. Once there were forests, and Moslem princes enjoyed hunting in them, but these have long since been cleared. Today, were it not for the efforts of local farmers and a number of projects sponsored by the governments of India and Pakistan, the Punjab might be a desert. In Roman times the Sahara had olive yards and orchards and was fertile, then goats were allowed to eat the bark from the trees, animal farmers neglected the cultivation of the land and the desert took over. What the Sahara did in north Africa the Thar could do in the Punjab were it not for the skill and industry of its farmers.

Farms are usually smallholdings of some twenty or thirty acres. Upon the death of a landowner the holding is divided between his sons, and this tends to keep them small. Often they are made up of widely scattered parcels of land and much time is spent travelling from one strip to another. The main crops are sugar cane, rice, cotton, oil seeds, millet and wheat. The Punjab has been called the granary of <u>India</u>.*

THE PUNJAB IS A LAND OF HISTORY

Since the Indo-Pakistan war of 1971, East Pakistan has been separate politically from West Pakistan and is now known as Bangla Desh. References in this book are to the state which existed prior to the secession.

One of the world's oldest civilisations grew up in the Indus Valley almost six thousand years ago. Mohenjo-daro and Harappa were its most famous cities. The site of the latter was on the bank of the river Ravi in the Punjab. Scholars are still attempting to understand the Indus Valley script and much of the story of this civilisation is still uncertain. It is only during the last fifty years that serious attempts have been made to study it.

The Indus Valley civilisation came to an end before Britain's Stonehenge was even built. The two-thousand-year-old culture probably fell before the Aryan invaders who entered north-west India from Uzbekistan sometime before 1700 B.C.E.

The following passage from the **Rig Veda**, one of the Hindu scriptures, may well be a poetic way of describing the conquest. The Dasa or 'dark people' is the Aryan name for the people of the Indus Valley. What they called themselves is not known.

To avoid confusion whenever India in any other sense than the present Republic of India is mentioned, it will be underlined thus.

'The chief wise god who as soon as born
   surpassed the gods in power;

Before whose vehemence the two worlds trembled
   by reason of the greatness of his valour: he,
   O men, is Indra.

Who made firm the quaking earth, who set at
   rest the agitated mountains;

Who measured out the air more widely, who
   supported heaven: he, O men, is Indra.

Who having slain the serpent released the seven
   streams, who drove the cows before the
   unclosing Vala,

Who between two rocks has produced fire,
   victor in battles: he, O men, is Indra.

By whom all things here have been made
   unstable, who has made subject the Dasa
   colour and has made it disappear;

Who as a gambler takes the stake has taken
   possession of the foe: he, O men, is Indra.'

The hymn refers to the seven streams. In ancient
times seven rivers, not five, did flow through the
Punjab and the pre-Aryan inhabitants did control
their flow with flood barriers. By breaking the dams
the Aryans may have used the river waters as a
weapon against the cities.

Harappa stood on the Ravi and is the most
famous city of this period in the Punjab to have
been excavated. Some archaeologists have
suggested that the invading Aryans intermarried
with the citizens of Harappa and that their fate may
not have been as terrible as the hymn states.

Cyrus, the Persian who allowed the Jewish
exiles to return from Babylon to Jerusalem,
extended his empire eastwards to the Indus, and
Darius the Great reached the Ganges. He found

India a wealthy country and derived much of his annual income from it. The Greek writer Herodotus states: 'the Indians, the most populous nation in the known world, paid the largest sum: 360 tabuts of gold dust'.

The rival of Persia was Greece and **Alexander the Great** marched into India after defeating Darius III. In 326 B.C.E. his army entered the Punjab. After four years of campaigning they were becoming discontented. Each victory took them farther away from Greece. At the river Beas Alexander questioned his generals, 'I observe, gentlemen, that when I would lead you on to a new venture you no longer follow me with your old spirit. I have asked you to meet me that we may come to a decision together. Are we upon my advice to go forward, or upon yours to turn back?' General Coenus spoke for the common soldiers and asked Alexander to head for home. Reluctantly Alexander turned back but not before he had sailed with part of his army to the mouth of the Indus— partly in the hope of discovering the source of the Nile. In 323 B.C.E. on the journey home he died of malaria in Babylon. He was only 33 years old.

The next famous name known to the west and important in the history of the Punjab is **Mohammed,** the great prophet and founder of Islam who died in 632 C.E. His work was confined to Arabia but within a century of his death followers of the Prophet had reached the river Loire in France and the province of Sind in India. It was now that the words India and Hindu came into use, as a term used by the Arabs to describe the non-Moslem country and its inhabitants which lay east of the Indus.

It was not until 1206 that Delhi was captured by the Moslems and their control of northern India was intermittent until **Babur's** campaigns in the Punjab in the 1520s. All uncertainty was removed and the era of the Mogul Emperors began. Guru Nanak, the founder of the Sikh religion, witnessed Babur's campaigns. One legend says that Nanak was imprisoned by the Emperor's troops and released on Babur's personal instructions. For two hundred years the Punjab was part of the Mogul Empire but with the death of Aurangzeb (1658–1707) another period of unsettled rule began. Control gradually passed to the Sikhs and during the reign of Ranjit Singh, the Lion of Punjab (1780–1839), it became a Sikh province.

MAHARAJA RANJIT SINGH OF LAHORE

Ranjit Singh, ruler of the Punjab from 1797 until 1839, is the popular hero of Sikh history, occupying something of the position which Robin Hood or Francis Drake hold in British folk history. His picture will sometimes be found in a Sikh home showing him riding his horse Lailh which he obtained from a Moslem prince.

The Maharaja was a small, ugly man, not the stuff that television heroes are made of. Smallpox had marked his face and destroyed his left eye. Once someone asked him 'Where were you when God was handing out good looks?' and he replied 'Seeking power!' He was an ambitious, courageous man who inspired his men to perform acts of great daring.

Power and wealth came his way and he turned the dream of an independent Sikh state into a reality. In 1809 he made a treaty with the British which he honoured for the rest of his life. It made him secure on his eastern frontier and so enabled him to look to the north and west for expansion. His forces occupied Kashmir, Multan and Peshawar. In 1813 he acquired the famous Koh-i-noor

diamond which can be seen in the Tower of
London as part of the Crown Jewels. In 1823 he
defeated the Afghans and dominated the north-west
frontier to the Khyber Pass.

Maharaja Ranjit Singh employed Moslems and
Europeans to build up his army and administration.
He also contributed to the decoration of the famous
Hindu Temple of Siva at Benares.

THE SIKHS UNDER BRITISH RULE

It took two wars and ten years for the British to
defeat the Sikhs after the death of Ranjit Singh.
Sikhs were often regarded as the fiercest opponents
the British ever had to face in India. Defeat came
partly because of the treachery of allies who had
not been happy under Sikh rule and, now that it
was crumbling, were looking to their own future.
Also a number of native rulers felt that the time
was ripe for them to join the British in the hope of
gaining wealth and land from the state which had
dominated them for so long.

Soon after the end of the war, in 1849, the British
began a number of irrigation projects in the Punjab
and such towns as Lyallpur arose. They also drafted
Sikhs into the British army, permitting them to keep
their beards and wear their turbans. In 1857 Sikhs
remained loyal to the British during the Indian
Mutiny.

In the Great War of 1914–1918 Sikhs fought for
Britain against the Germans and the Turks, but
as the war had come to an end a long series of
troubles began in India. The Sikhs were involved
in two of the many incidents. In April 1919 at Jallianwala Bagh in Amritsar a demonstrating crowd
refused to disperse and General Dyer ordered his
troops to open fire. Fifteen hundred people were
killed or wounded. Many of them were Sikhs. The
effect upon the Indians was to shock them as much

as the Sharpeville massacre in South Africa shocked the world thirty years later, and to make them intensify the struggle for independence. The Amritsar mob had also lynched a white nurse, and the British government ordered citizens who passed the spot to crawl on their stomachs. Humiliation only increased anger.

Disputes over the possession and management of **Gurdwaras** in the Punjab dragged on for five years and caused added friction between the British and the Sikhs.

Mahatma Gandhi is only one of the famous names in the recent story of Indian independence; Jinnah, the Moslem, Nehru, and **Baba Kharak Singh**, the Sikh, are others. Until the Second World War they struggled and during it they did not let up. Many Sikhs, a traditional source of man-power in the British army, were unwilling to fight to preserve an Empire which refused freedom. Other Sikhs fought against Germany and Japan.

After the war it became clear that the European Empires of France, Holland and Britain could not survive. Those who had just preserved their own liberty could not refuse it to others, though sometimes the Europeans gave up their power reluctantly. On August 15th, 1947 the British Empire of India became the dominions of India and Pakistan. The Punjab was partitioned. The Sikhs who had hoped for their independent Punjab dominion found themselves divided between the two new nations of India and Pakistan. 62% of the land and 55% of the population of the Punjab went to Pakistan.

INDEPENDENCE AND THE PUNJAB

The Punjab has been torn in two. Half of

the Punjab of Ranjit Singh now belongs to Pakistan, the rest is within the Republic of India.

For many years the people of the subcontinent had been demanding independence from Britain; eventually it was agreed that this should be granted but that there should be two nations, not one, Pakistan and India. Sir Cyril Radcliffe headed a commission which was given the unenviable task of determining a frontier where no previous boundary had existed. A Sikh historian, Khushwant Singh, has written, 'The Radcliffe award was as fair as it could be to the Moslems and Hindus. The one community to which no boundary award could have done justice without doing injustice to others were the Sikhs. Their richest lands, over one hundred and fifty historical shrines and half their population were left on the Pakistan side of the dividing line.'

The story of what happened when the Punjab was divided in two and the Sikh homeland broken up must now be told. It is an important episode in Sikh history, especially as they hoped to become a separate independent state, but it is one from which no one, Moslem, Hindu, Sikh or Briton, emerges with any credit. Perhaps we shall feel sympathy for the Sikh but decide that, given the fact that India was going to become two states, there could have been no other consequence.

While Lord Mountbatten, the last Viceroy of India, was handing over power to the new governments of the dominions of India and Pakistan, civil war was raging in the Punjab. In a fortnight almost 1,000 of the inhabitants of Amritsar were murdered. Villages were burnt down and the roads became choked with refugees.

On the day of independence the frontier between the two new nations, in the Punjab area, was still undecided. Three days later details of the partitioning of the Punjab were given in 'The Times' which two days later, on August 20th, carried the following report:

'About 70,000 Moslems have arrived in Lahore during the past few days from Amritsar, now in the province of East Punjab, and 40,000 of them have been accommodated in camps opened by the West Punjab Government. At least 70% of the Sikh and Hindu population is believed to have left Lahore in the past four months. According to one estimate not more than 10,000 of a former Hindu and Sikh population of over three hundred thousand are left in the city.'

This extract reduces a story of agony, suffering and cruelty covering many months and about six million people to a few lines.

Khushwant Singh states that 4,351,477 Hindus and Sikhs moved from the North-West Frontier Province and West Punjab and 4,286,755 Moslems went in the other direction from East Punjab. He claims that the Hindus and Sikhs left 67 **lakh** acres of good land and the Moslems 47 **lakh** acres of poorer land.

Figures mean very little. We may know what 1,000 or even 2,000 look like because we have seen a whole school assembled. Those who have been to an FA Cup Final have been part of a crowd of 100,000. We are thinking of two groups forty times as great moving in opposite directions, often on the same roads.

The Sikhs organised themselves into armed bands (**jathas**) to clear the East Punjab of Moslems, while Sikh and Hindu refugees fleeing from West Punjab (now Pakistan) were harassed by Moslems.

Gradually the refugees reached safety and the long task of resettling them and establishing peace began.

THE PUNJAB TODAY

India is a country in which many changes are taking place. Whenever Kishan talks to friends who have been to India they tell him of them and discuss the the future of the country.

India's problems are great; the westerner can scarcely begin to understand them. In 1951 it had a a population of 357 million, in 1961 439 million, and now 550 million. This means that every ten years the number of people to be fed, housed and employed rises by more than there are in the whole of the British Isles.

It seems almost impossible to solve such a problem and no one can envy the Prime Minister and Government of India their task.

Efforts are being made to increase the amount of land under cultivation and, by better farming methods, to improve the yield per acre. If India can produce more herself and so have to spend less of her income importing food and raw materials she will have gone a considerable way towards solving her balance-of-payments problem.

As we have seen already, much of India's farming depends on irrigation. The key to this is ensuring a secure water supply. No one has yet found a way of controlling the monsoons; so far as the Punjab is concerned, the Bhakra-Nangal project is the next best thing.

Work began on a series of dams on the river Sutlej soon after India became independent. The main dam is the Bhakra dam 740 feet high, 14 feet higher than the Hoover Dam in the USA, which used to be the world's highest. Eight miles farther downstream is the Nangal dam, only 95 feet high but over three hundred metres long. The lake behind this dam, besides other things, provides water for an irrigation canal forty miles long.

The project provides electricity for Delhi and

many towns in the Punjab, and water to irrigate over 3 million acres of land which could not be cultivated twenty years ago. We cannot imagine what 3 million acres means; but it may help if we remember that this is about the size of the West and North Ridings of Yorkshire put together or double the size of Lincolnshire or Devon.

Last year Kishan's father with other Sikhs from Leeds and Birmingham paid a charter-flight visit to the Punjab, staying for a month. He told his friends of the changes he had seen—irrigation wells with concreted sides and brick parapets; channels leading from them which were brick-lined, no longer rough cuttings through the earth. He had seen many Persian wheels still driven by oxen or camel but an increasing number were powered by oil pumps.

Electricity has come to many of the villages in the Punjab, and tarmac roads are replacing cart tracks. Largely because of the refugee problem which followed the partition, and the traditions of dividing the land among their sons, holdings are small. A small-scale farmer could not afford a tractor but when many relatives live together in a village they can often combine to buy a family tractor and in the same way obtain a lorry. With the help of the Indian government many Sikhs who used to live in west Punjab are now pioneering in the one-time deserts opened up to cultivation by the Bhakra-Nangal project just as their grandparents first worked the newly irrigated land around Lyallpur under the British Raj one hundred years ago. Sikhs in Britain help by sending money to their relatives back home.

It will be many years before the thatch-roof, mud-hut picture of India, with children helping their father to plough the field with the family ox, becomes completely a thing of the past, but that picture is growing more untrue every day, especially in the Punjab. Sikhs living in Britain try to return to their home districts in India every five years or so. Each time they return the change shocks them. The Punjab has come a long way since 1947.

A PROJECT WORK

These are some of the things you might do now that you have read this chapter.

1. *Collect information from geography books about the various methods of irrigation in use in different parts of the world. In particular try to discover the origin of the Persian wheel and the way it works. You may be able to find a picture of one.*
2. *Cyrus, Darius the Great and Alexander are among the greatest names in world history. What do your history books tell you about them? How large was Alexander the Great's Empire when he died in 323 B.C.E.?*
3. *Through Mohammed one of the world's greatest religions came into existence. Write a brief biography of Mohammed. On a map show the spread of Islam between 623 and 732 C.E. In which countries is Islam the main religion today?*

4. *Trace the story of Britain in India to 1849 when the Punjab was annexed.*

5. *Your local reference library may have a photo-copy of 'The Times' for August 1947; from it you will be able to read the story of this troubled period in the history of the Punjab for yourself.*

6. **Book and Poster Exhibition.** *With the help of other school departments and the librarian gather together as many books about India as you can. Try to obtain posters and maps from travel agencies. Don't forget to give a special place to the Punjab, the home of the Sikhs.*

7. **Stamp Exhibition.** *India and Pakistan have issued stamps depicting discoveries made in the Indus Valley. Other stamps commemorate famous Sikh leaders, a few illustrated in this book.*
   The greatness of Persia and ancient Greece is also shown on stamps.
   It should be possible to mount an exhibition based on the chapter you have just read. Begin by consulting a stamp catalogue.
   You will need to provide explanatory notes and to protect the stamps from grubby fingers!

4

THE BEGINNINGS OF THE SIKH RELIGION

Mr. Ruprai invited Alan to visit the Sikh Temple one Sunday so that he could see and listen to the the service. First he went to Kishan's home.

"Before you come," Mr. Ruprai said, "we had better tell you about our religion, how it began and the stories of its greatest leaders."

Kishan was listening too, and Alan looked surprised. Mr. Ruprai smiled.

"You are wondering why Kishan should want to know about our religion as well as you, Alan?"

"Well, if you must know, I was," Alan replied.

"May I ask you one question in reply, Alan? Do you know everything about the history of your religion, Christianity?"

Alan thought for a moment.

"Well, no, not really. We learned about the Old Testament and the life of Jesus at school, but nothing much since that time."

Mr. Ruprai nodded.

"Just so. It is much the same with our faith. There is so much to know that many of us are still learning more and more as we get older, and as you shall hear, we have had not one, but ten religious teachers, each of whom has contributed something to our religion."

Kishan turned towards Alan, smiling broadly.

"So you see, Alan, even *I* don't know everything."

Alan just grinned, and they sat back to listen as Kishan's father began to tell them the exciting story of the Sikh faith.

He began by mentioning two words, **guru** and **chela**. **Guru** means spiritual teacher. **Chela** is the name given to his pupil. It has always been usual in India for a young man to attach himself to a **guru** who will teach him the meaning of the scriptures and the methods of meditation. A whole section of the Hindu Scriptures, called the Upanishads, is really a compilation of such teachings.

When Jesus gathered his disciples around him and taught them the Lord's Prayer and other things he was behaving rather like an Indian **guru**.

One of the most recent famous gurus has been the Maharishi Mahesh Yogi. One of the earliest known by name was Siddartha Gautama, the Buddha.

The founder of the Sikh religion, Nanak, was a man of this sort. Seekers after truth, both Hindu and Moslem, came to him, listened to his teaching and he became their guru. By the time of his death he had so many disciples that he felt it necessary to designate a successor. It is unlikely that Guru Nanak intended to found a new religion but as time went on the disciples, or Sikhs as they came to be called, became increasingly distinct from both Hindu and Moslem.

There were ten gurus in all and by the time of the last, Sikhism had become an independent religion.

In the 170 years between the death of Guru Nanak and the death of the tenth Guru many changes in the faith and practice of the new community took place. For example Nanak had been a pacifist but from the time of the fifth Guru Sikhs were often persecuted and eventually accepted the view that religious liberty should be defended by the sword.

However, each guru believed that through him Nanak continued to reveal the truth of God. In their writings they frequently used Nanak's name, not their own, and so far as doctrine is concerned it is true to say that Sikhism is based on his teaching.

Each guru after Nanak was chosen by his predecessor on the basis of merit not kinship.

Before his death Guru Nanak chose his friend and disciple Lehna to be his successor and gave him the name Angad, which means 'my own body'. This little incident may help us to understand the work of the ten gurus. Each teacher was building upon the foundation of Nanak and often in their hymns they use his name and not their own—as though it was Nanak who is speaking. Each guru in turn appointed his successor until the tenth, Guru Gobind Singh, assembled the most important teachings and declared that they were complete. After him there would be no further human teacher; the Guru would now be the book, the **Granth**. It says something for his humility that he permitted none of his own hymns to be included in it.

The Guru Granth Sahib (The Book) being carried into the Gurdwara in Bradford at its ceremonial opening in March, 1972.

Portraits of all ten gurus are kept in the **Gurdwara** or Temple.

THE BEGINNINGS OF THE SIKH RELIGION

1. Guru Nanak 1469–1539
2. Guru Angad 1504–1552
3. Guru Amar Das 1479–1574
4. Guru Ram Das 1534–1581
5. Guru Arjan 1563–1606
6. Guru Har Gobind 1595–1645
7. Guru Har Rai 1630–1661
8. Guru Kar Krishan 1656–1664
9. Guru Tegh Bahadur 1621–1675
10. Guru Gobind Singh 1666–1708

Mr. Ruprai had come to the end of his talk about the Sikh faith.

"I will show you the portraits of the gurus in our Gurdwara when you come, Alan, and try and tell you something about each one. I think you'll find that it will be very interesting."

Both boys nodded. They knew that they would look forward to that. The next chapter tells you what Mr. Ruprai had to tell them when they finally saw the portraits for themselves.

5

THE TEN GURUS

GURU NANAK (1469–1539)

Sometimes Moslem and Hindu have lived in peace, more often they have been enemies, if not openly at war at least unable to agree. Today they cannot agree who shall rule Kashmir, and the Punjab is constantly in danger. The worst danger it could face would not be war, but the threat of India or Pakistan to dam or divert the head waters of the five rivers in their own interest and to the harm of the other. Fortunately the two governments have made a treaty agreement on the use of the waters of the Punjab.

There have always been some men who have lived and even died to bring Hindu and Moslem together. One, very recently, was Mohandas Karamchand Gandhi. He was assassinated on January 30th 1948 by a fellow Hindu who was opposed to Gandhi's attempts to reconcile Hindus and Moslems and to his demands that Moslems in India should receive fair treatment.

Centuries ago two other men worked to the same end. They were Kabir (1440–1518) and Nanak (1469–1539). Kabir came from Benares, his parents were Hindus and his teaching was accepted by Hindus and Moslems.

Nanak was the son of an accountant though of the Kshatrya, or warrior caste, and was born in the Punjab. His home village of Talwandi, now called Nankana Sahib, near Lahore, was largely Hindu but had a Moslem zamindar (landholder). He was eventually employed by Daulat Khan Lodi, the Afghan Moslem governor of the provine

Nanak was clearly used to Hindu and Moslem living together. He was also familiar with the ideas of the two great religions and was deeply influenced by them both. However, he did not try to take elements from

THE TEN GURUS

both religions and create a third.

Nanak's aim was to proclaim the truth which lies behind religion, and so he rejected Hinduism and Islam as he experienced them, saying 'Neither the Veda nor the Koran know the mystery'. What he meant was that it is not enough to know the scriptures; God himself can be known only in the heart. This is a real knowledge.

Of Hindu ritual Nanak wrote:

'Gods and goddesses are worshipped but what can one ask them and what can they give? The idols are washed with water but they sink in water and so are useless vessels to carry you across the Ocean of Existence.'

'The Hindus have forgotten God, and are going the wrong way.

They worship according to the instruction of the sage.

They are blind and dumb, the blindest of the blind.

They ignorantly take stones and worship them.

O Hindus, how shall the stone which sinks carry you across?'

He was opposed to the Hindu caste system and said 'Perceive in all men the light of God. Do not ask a man's caste for in the hereafter there is no caste.'

'Caste and status are futile, for the One watches over all. If anyone exalts himself, the true measure of his dignity will be revealed when his record is produced in the court of the Lord.'

Islam fared no better. Bhai Gurdas, his biographer, narrates that Nanak once went to Mecca and at night went to sleep with his feet towards the Ka'aba. The Moslems were furious at

Nanak's irreverence. "Take my feet, then, and point them in the direction where God is not", said the Guru.

Hypocrites of all kinds came in for criticism:

'He who sings songs about God without understanding them; who converts his house into a mosque to satisfy his hunger; who being unemployed has his ears pierced so that he can beg as a yogi; who calls himself a teacher of truth (a **guru** or a **pir**) but goes about begging; do not pay respect to such a man. The man who earns his bread by the sweat of his brow and gives some to others, he it is who knows the true way of life.'

The Guru regarded man's treatment of women as hypocritical and wrong. When a Hindu died his widow would show the completeness of her devotion by performing the act of *sati* (or *suttee*), that is being burned with his body on the funeral pyre. Nanak would have nothing to do with this. Moslem women often lived a lonely secluded life in purdah. Nanak disapproved of this too.

He believed in the equality of women as a verse of his shows:

'By woman we are conceived and from her we are
    born;
With her we are betrothed and with her married,
It is woman who is our friend and she who
    perpetuates the family.
When one woman dies, man seeks another
And with her he is established in society.
Out of woman comes woman herself: without her
    no other exists.
Why call woman evil when she gives birth to
    kings?'

Nanak travelled to the great pilgrimage centres but had no time for those who went with impure hearts and expected the action in itself to do them some good.

'If anyone goes to bathe at a place of pilgrimage with an evil heart and the body of a thief, one part (the outside) is cleansed by the bathing but the other (the heart) becomes even filthier. Outwardly he is washed like a **faqir's** begging bowl, but inside he is poison and impurity. A **sadhu** possesses goodness even if he does not bathe and a thief, even if he bathes, remains a thief.'

Sometimes, as when he was found sleeping with his feet towards the Ka'aba, Nanak would try to provoke people to think not by words but by actions.

Once at Hardwar, a town on the Ganges, Nanak saw the pilgrims standing in the river and throwing water into the air, in the direction of the rising sun. The Guru began splashing water in the opposite direction and was soon asked for an explanation.

Instead of giving them an answer he asked them to explain what they were doing.

"We are sending water to our ancestors in heaven."

"And I am watering my fields near Lahore", said Nanak.

The pilgrims laughed at him scornfully but he replied, "Your ancestors are farther away than my farm and yet you say your water will reach them. Why shouldn't the water I throw reach my farm in the Punjab? You can only honour the memory of your dead by doing good deeds. In this way you pay them real respect."

The cow is a sacred animal to the Hindus. They will not eat beef and many, in fact, will not eat meat of any animal or of a fish or even eggs, as these possess life. Moslems, like the Jews, regard the pig as 'unclean' and will not eat pork.

Nanak refused to believe that what entered a man's stomach could affect him spiritually.

Once, a young friend shot a deer and gave it to Nanak who gave instructions how it should be cooked. Hindus present were offended and angered. Nanak reminded them that there was life in the food grains they ate as well as in animals and that the water they depended upon was teeming with life and was the source of life. They sacrificed animals, they were made of flesh themselves, how could flesh be evil?

Nanak did not want to destroy men's faith and certainly he did not regard Hinduism and Islam as false, but he knew that true religion was something inward, not an outward show.

Therefore, he once taught a group of Moslems:
'Let compassion be your mosque,
Let faith be your prayer mat,
Let honest living be your Koran,
Let modesty be the rules of observance,
Let piety be the fasts you keep,
And in such ways strive to become a Moslem.
Right conduct the Ka'aba; Truth the Prophet,
Good deeds your prayer;
Submission to the Lord's will your rosary;
If you do this the Lord will be your Protector.'

In his late fifties Nanak settled with his family at Kartarpur, on the bank of the river Ravi, on land which a rich man had given him. Kartarpur means 'abode of the Creator', or the Holy City.

Now men who shared his views came to Nanak,

both Hindus and Moslems. They called him the King of holy men and composed this rhyme:

'Baba Nanak sah fakir
Hindu ka guru, musalman ka pir.'

(Nanak is the king of Holy men,
Guru of Hindus, Pir of Moslems.)

The community of disciples never dreamed that this was the beginning of a new religion as they shared their common life together. In fact Nanak was not attempting to found the world's youngest religion, he was merely trying to call men of all faiths to the true service of God, but he had laid the foundation of a faith whose home would be in the Punjab among Hindus and Moslems.

Nanak was a reformer who found himself with so many followers that before he died he had to choose his successor.

He was also a poet, and one of the tasks of the second Guru was to collect his verses. There are 974 of them in the Guru Granth. The most famous is the **Japji** which is sung at morning prayer and means Meditation. It begins:

'There is one God
Eternal Truth is His Name,
Maker of all things,
Fearing nothing and hating nothing,
Immortal, Unborn, Self, Existent:
By the grace of the Guru made known to men.'

The whole poem is a meditation upon God who is the truth:

'As He was in the beginning, the Truth,
So throughout all ages
He has been the Truth,
So even now He is the Truth immanent,
So forever and ever He shall be the Truth eternal.'

It is the opening hymn of the Sikh scriptures. (You will find out more about the **Guru Granth Sahib** on p. 59).

Mr. Ruprai told Alan an interesting story which, he said, showed how both Hindus and Moslems respected the founder of the Sikh faith.

Just before Nanak died many of his disciples gathered round him. Those who were Hindus asked that they might cremate his body; the Moslems asked permission to bury it according to their own custom. Guru Nanak told them each to place bunches of flowers at the side of him. "When I am dead, those whose flowers remain in bloom may do with my body according to their custom."

In the morning they returned to find both lots of flowers blooming—but Nanak's body had gone!

This story is a myth, that is a story with a meaning. The events in a myth may or may not have happened, what is important is its significance.

What is the meaning of this story?

Many religions, including Christianity, have their myths. Can you think of some and try to discover what assertions they are making?

B   PROJECT WORK

One of the **Janam Sakhis** (*biographies*) *of Guru Nanak has the description of an experience of Guru Nanak.*

'One day Nanak went to the river and removing his clothes left them in the care of a servant. While he was bathing messengers of God came and he was transported by them to the divine court. There he was

given a cup of nectar (**amrit**) and with it came the command, 'Nanak, this is the cup of My Name (**Nam**). Drink it.' This he did and was charged to go into the world and preach the divine Name.

In the meantime the servant had become anxious at his master's failure to emerge from the water. He returned to the town and informed Daulat Khan (a local Moslem official and Nanak's employer). He rode out at once and had the river dragged, but Nanak's body was not found. Three days later, however, the missing Nanak suddenly re-appeared at the point where his body had entered the river. Daulat Khan joined the crowd which gathered, but Guru Nanak evidently remained silent, for the people explained to the Nawab that he had sustained injury in the river. Hearing this Daulat Khan departed with a heavy heart and Nanak went with Mardana to live with some **faqirs**.

For one day Nanak maintained his silence and then on the following day he spoke, saying "There is neither Hindu nor Mussulman" (*Moslem*).

You might like to discuss this experience and the story which contains it.

The Buddha, Jesus, St. Paul and Mohammed and many others have had similar experiences. Try to assemble a collection of such narratives and compare them.

THE SIKH LANGUAGE IS WRITTEN DOWN
GURU ANGAD (1504-1552)

To succeed Guru Nanak would not be easy. To
make it possible, he publicly declared that his mantle
had fallen upon Lehna or, as he expressed it, Lehna
is now Angad—'my own body'. Before his death
Nanak instructed another Sikh, Bhai Buddha (Bhai
means brother) to put the saffron mark upon
Angad's forehead to proclaim him the second Guru
for he had the same light and the same ways. The
Guru merely changed his body.

Angad went from Kartarpur to another village
named Khadur, where his home was. By now there
were Sikhs in a number of places following the
ways of the Guru and instructing others. He saw
the need for writing down the hymns of Nanak but
immediately he was faced with a problem. No one
had ever tried to put the language into a written
form. There had been no need. Farmers, smiths,
weavers and tanners had no use for writing; they
learned by doing, and fathers taught their children
to follow their trade. Tax collectors and accountants
in offices needed to be able to write. Nanak could
write, otherwise he would not have been employed
by Daulat Khan.

Angad worked on scripts used by accountants
and money-lenders and eventually produced a
written form of Punjabi. He called the script
Gurmukhi, the language of the Guru. Once it had
been produced Nanak's hymns were written down
and copies sent to the growing number of Sikh
communities and from this time on the poems of
Angad and his successors were also recorded.

The importance of Guru Angad's work cannot be
overstressed.

The holy books of the Hindus, the Vedas,
Upanishads and Gita were in Sanskrit, which very
few could read, and of those most were members

of the Brahmin caste. Most Hindus had to rely on the priests or the village storyteller, or tales learned at their mothers' knees as children, for any religious knowledge they had. No wonder Nanak found superstition and ritualism without understanding among the Hindus of his day! The Koran is the sacred book of Islam. It was written in Arabic, which few Moslems in India could read. They had to depend upon a mullah for their religious education. Because of Guru Angad's work the Sikhs were independent, each could read the teachings of the Guru for himself. It was written in his own language But of course, very few Sikhs could read.

Guru Angad set to work providing education for the children of the communities. The school textbook was the written hymns of Guru Nanak.

Ever since the time of Angad Sikhs have set a high value upon education.

GURU AMAR DAS (1479–1574)

Not many men have deserved the title 'great' and sometimes the word has been used to describe men who were cruel and harmed people, seldom doing any good. One truly great emperor was Akbar. He ruled in India 400 years ago from 1556 to 1605 at almost the same time as Queen Elizabeth I. He was a Moslem, but Hindus and Sikhs lived in his land and he wished them to live in peace and worship in freedom as they chose. Akbar was a seeker after truth throughout his life and would travel far and wide to talk with sincere men and listen to their teaching about God.

Amar Das, the third Guru of the Sikhs, was a great friend of Akbar and like Guru Nanak he was respected by Moslems and Hindus alike. Guru Nanak had set up what he called a 'temple of bread' where men brought corn and fuel and worked together for the good of the community. To it the poor could come and find food and work. His successor continued this, and the free kitchen where all could eat together was called the **Langar**. Amar Das made the **Langar** an institution so that wherever there is a Sikh Temple a room is set aside where guests can be fed, and where they can spend the night if they need to. In this way Sikhs show that everyone is their brother. To show that all men were equal the gurus would serve in the **Langar** and take their own meals there. They also insisted that any visitors should do the same. Moslems and Hindus who were their friends must put aside their differences and eat food together. Akbar was no exception. When he visited Guru Amar Das he was not treated differently from anyone else. He sat among the poor and the travel-stained, sharing their simple food. Then he went to talk with the guru. In the **Langar** he learned to be humble and only a humble man could hear the voice of God. It is said that the motto of Guru Amar Das was **'Pehle Pengat Piche Sangat'**, which means 'First sit in a row in the kitchen, then seek the company of the Guru'.

For twenty-two years Amar Das led the Sikhs, dying at the age of ninety-five. "Do good to others by giving good advice, by setting a good example, and by always having the welfare of mankind in your heart", he preached. No one ever followed that preaching more faithfully than the Guru himself. He was a saintly man but he also had a sense of humour. One day a jealous man who thought he was better fitted to be the leader of the Sikhs kicked the stool Amar Das was sitting on from underneath him. As the Guru fell to the floor he looked at the man and exclaimed "You must have hurt your foot!" The man scowled and left the room

THE FOUNDER OF THE HOLY CITY:
GURU RAM DAS (1534–1581)

Both Angad and Amar Das were brought up in
Hindu homes and only accepted the teachings of
Guru Nanak as adults. By 1574 when Ram Das
became Guru there were many men and women in
the **Sangat** who had learned the teachings of Guru
Nanak at their mothers' knees. Guru Ram Das,
son-in-law of the third Guru, and his wife Bibi
Bhani, were two such people.

Ram Das was aware that the teachings of Guru
Nanak would have a permanent place in the Punjab.
His words, the **Gurbani**, as Sikhs call them,
would be passed from one generation to another
as Ram Das and his wife were teaching them to
their children. Sikhism was spreading but it had no
centre. Nanak's community had been at Kartarpur
on the Ravi, Angad's at Khadur and Amar Das's
at Goindwal. Ram Das took the decision to found a
city on the land which the Emperor Akbar had
given his wife. He invited merchants and traders
to market their goods there and soon a thriving
community grew up. Men gave the city the name of
the Guru, **Guru Ka Chak**, others used the form
Chak Ram Das or **Ram Das Pura** but all had the
the same meaning.

Today the city is called **Amritsar**, the pool of
nectar, after the lake which surrounds the central
Gurdwara of Sikhism, and it has a population of
more than 400,000 (roughly as many as Bristol or
Edinburgh).

THE BUILDER OF THE GOLDEN TEMPLE:
GURU ARJAN (1563–1606)

Once the Sikhs possessed a city it was only to be
expected that they would build a **Gurdwara** in it

and that it would become the Holy Place of the Sikhs. The **Gurdwara** is the focal point of any Sikh community whether it be in Vancouver, Southall, Leeds or the Punjab. It represents the two great principles of Sikhism, the worship of God and the brotherhood of man.

Sikhism was emerging more and more clearly as an independent religion and Guru Arjan himself wrote:

'I will not worship with the Hindu
Or like the Moslem go to Mecca.
I shall serve Him and no other.
I will not pray to idols or say the Moslem prayer.
I shall put my heart at the feet of the One
   Supreme Being
For we are neither Hindus nor Moslems.'

Yet Arjan still saw the way of Nanak as a bridge between Hindu and Moslem. The architecture of the Golden Temple was a blending of Hindu and Moslem styles. Also symbolic of his hopes was the fact that he asked Mian Mir, a Moslem respected by all men, to lay the foundation stone. The Temple was begun in 1589 and soon completed Sikhs called it the **Har Mandar**, the Lord's Abode. It was built with steps leading down to it not up to it as many Hindu temples and Christian Churches have. As Guru Arjan put it, this was to ensure that even the person of the very lowest cast had to go even lower, that is humble himself still further, to meet the Guru. Unlike a Hindu Temple it had four doors to show that it was open to all four castes. Some mosques are closed to non-Moslems and even today quite illegally, Harijans (Gandhi's name for untouchables, meaning 'Children of God') are prevented from entering some Hindu

Temples. All men and women of all faiths may enter the Golden Temple. The Har Mandar is open to everyone.

The Golden Temple as it stands is the work of Maharaja Ranjit Singh who had the following inscription put on it:

'The Great Guru in His wisdom looked upon
Maharaja Ranjit Singh as His chief servant
And Sikh, and in His benevolence bestowed
On him the privilege of serving the Temple.'

In 1604 Bhai Gurdas, on Guru Arjan's instructions, completed a collection of the hymns of the Sikh Gurus, plus some compositions of Moslems and Hindus, including untouchables, and this became the sacred book of the Sikhs. It was installed in the **Har Mandar** and Bhai Buddha was first reader or **Granthi**.

Eleven miles from Amritsar, at Taran Taran, which means 'pool of salvation' Guru Arjan started a leprosarium. It is well known that in medieval England lepers had to warn people of their approach by ringing a hand-bell and shouting 'Unclean, Unclean', and the story of Father Damien, the Belgian priest who worked among lepers, contracted their illness and died of it is also famous. Lepers have always been outcasts and untouchables in any society. We should not be surprised to discover the Sikhs who opposed the caste system caring for lepers.

Guru Arjan became the first Sikh martyr. It happened in this way. The great Mogul Emperor Akbar died in 1606. He had been a tolerant and kind ruler, listening to the views of all men. The Sikhs had prospered during his reign, receiving land and revenues. He had known and respected Amar Das, Ram Das and Arjan. When the **Granth** had been compiled mischief makers at his court told Akbar

it was an anti-Moslem book and encouraged him
to destroy it and persecute the Sikhs. Wisely he
refused to listen to rumour but went to Amritsar
the next time he was in the province and asked to
see the book. Bhai Buddha and Bhai Gurdas
brought it to him and read passages from it. He
showed his approval by a gift of money, by
providing the two disciples and Arjan with robes
of honour and at the Guru's request he remitted
the annual taxes of the district which had been
hard hit by the failure of the monsoons.

Akbar was succeeded by Jehangir, a very
different man. A revolt broke out in favour of his
son and when it had been suppressed he showed
no mercy to those he believed to have been
accomplices. Those who were jealous of the
Sikhs were quick to accuse Arjan, who was heavily
fined. He refused to pay the fine and denied the
charge of treason. After the arrest he was taken
to Lahore and condemned to death by torture,
although the Moslem holy man Mian Mir pleaded for
him. He drowned in the river Ravi, his body
was carried away by the currents and never
recovered. The date was May 30th 1606.

THE FIRST WARRIOR GURU:
HAR GOBIND (1595–1645)

Before he died Arjan managed to let his followers
know that his eleven-year-old son Har Gobind should
be his successor. Bhai Buddha installed him and
he and Bhai Gurdas advised the young leader in
his youth. He led the Sikhs for thirty-eight years
and his death was one of the few peaceful events
in his life.

'My rosary shall be the sword belt', he said when he became Guru. In that belt he wore two swords, one symbolising spiritual power, the other temporal. He built a castle at Amritsar, called Lohgarh (the castle of steel) and trained a small army. His pleasure, like that of a Mogul prince, was hunting and he told his followers that gifts of arms and horses were as acceptable as money.

Har Gobind accepted the title '**Sacha Padsah**' (the true Emperor). Not only in his love of hunting was he like a Mogul Emperor, he also held court sitting on a throne, sent envoys to ruling princes and welcomed their ambassadors. When he went on a journey a royal umbrella was held over his head and he had an armed retinue.

Not surprisingly the sixth Guru wrote no hymns, but he was faithful in his religious observance and knew the hymns of the **Granth** well.

It is more surprising that he was able to remain alive during the reign of Jehangir, who had been responsible for his father's death. He was arrested by the Emperor and imprisoned at Gwalior for over a year because, of course, the Sikhs had not paid the fine imposed on Arjan and the army was a threat to Mogul rule. Sikhs came to the prison and stood outside the walls of the fort in prayer and it seems that at last Jehangir took pity on the Guru, then probably sixteen years old, and ordered his release. More cautiously than before Har Gobind re-established the small army he had been compelled to disband. One writer says he had eight hundred horses in his stable and three hundred horsemen besides sixty men equipped with firearms.

In one way or another Har Gobind survived Jehangir's reign. One account suggests that the two men became friends and that the Guru once saved the Emperor from a tiger during a hunting expedition. The story is in keeping with Har Gobind's character but it is probably not true.

Shah Jahan succeeded Jehangir in 1627 and soon the Sikhs and Moguls were at war. The fighting took the form of skirmishes, ambushes and raids rather than pitched battles, for the Sikhs would have been heavily outnumbered and wiped out had the larger forces of Shah Jahan ever caught them in open country.

On one occasion a Moslem force came to arrest the Guru and arrived to find preparations being made for his daughter's wedding. Some cooks were killed, others fled and the feast was eaten by the intruders. On the way back to their headquarters the Moslems, who had eaten too much to fight well, were ambushed by Sikhs.

For much of this time Guru Har Gobind lived on the wooded foothills of the Himalayas at a place called Kiratpur. He became something of a folk-hero like Robin Hood, Hereward the Wake or Robert Bruce in British history, inspiring not only Sikhs but Hindus of the Punjab and tribesmen of Kashmir in the struggle with their Mogul overlords.

GURU HAR RAI (1630–1661)

Most of Guru Har Gobind's children died during his lifetime and neither of the two remaining sons seemed a suitable successor, though one, Tegh Bahadur, eventually became ninth Guru. Instead Har Gobind chose his grandson, then aged fourteen

He was a peaceful man and at any other period of history might have proved himself a second Angad. He once said 'You can repair a temple or a mosque but not a broken heart', and he would have liked to reorganise the communities

of Amritsar, Goindwal, Kartarpur and Khadur.
Instead, with his army of perhaps as many as
2,000 men, he was even compelled to leave Kiratpur
for a remote hill-village.

He became friendly with a son of the Mogul
Emperor, but when his father died this son lost the
war of succession to his brother Aurangzeb and
Sikh hopes of peace were dashed. Instead Ram Rai,
the Guru's son, was held hostage at the court of
the new Emperor in Delhi.

Before his death Guru Har Rai decided that his
younger son should succeed him.

GURU HARI KRISHEN (1656–1664)

'Pity the land where a child is king', is a saying from
English history, but it is true of any nation in which
it is the function of the king to rule and not simply
be a constitutional monarch. Emperor Aurangzeb
was not pleased with the tactics of Har Rai. He
wanted the succession of Ram Rai and summoned
five-year-old Hari Krishen to Delhi.

The small boy contracted smallpox but before his
death he told the people about him that the next
Guru was to be found in Bakala. This was the
village of his great-uncle Tegh Bahadur.

THE SECOND MARTYR GURU :
TEGH BAHADUR (1621–1675)

The ninth Guru accepted his position but with
great reluctance. He had not disputed his father's

decision twenty years earlier and had no wish for power or to be a leader.

He seems to have been very much like Nanak or Amar Das.

One of his poems (his son included 115 of them in the **Granth**) reads:

'That man who in the midst of grief is free from
    grieving,
And free from fear and free from the snare of
    delight,
Nor is covetous of gold that he knows to be dust,
Who is neither a backbiter nor a flatterer,
Nor has greed in his heart, nor vanity, nor any
    worldly attachment,
Who remains unmoved (*at his centre*) by good
    and ill fortune,
Who is indifferent to the world's praise and
    blame
And discards every wishful fantasy
Accepting his lot disinterestedly,
Nor worked upon by lust or anger,
God lives in such a man;
The man on whom the Grace of the Guru alights
Understands the way of conduct:
His soul, O Nanak, is mingled with the Lord
As water mingles with water!'

This was fortunately the spirit of Tegh Bahadur. No lesser man could have survived.

Aurangzeb, as we have seen, wanted Ram Rai to be Guru. He was unlikely to give Tegh Bahadur much peace. Also the Sikhs were divided among themselves. Some favoured the Emperor's favourite as a way of avoiding trouble. Others were looking for another Har Gobind to unite them against Aurangzeb. Tegh Bahadur was neither friend of the Emperor nor soldier. It seemed no one wanted him.

When he arrived at the Har Mandar at Amritsar the doors were slammed in his face. There was even a plot to murder him. He built a home of his own where he hoped to find peace—and even called it Anandpur, the house of peace but he found no peace there and had to leave the Punjab altogether. He went to Patna where, on December 26th 1666, his famous son Gobind Rai was born. From there he paid visits to Sikh communities in Bengal.

His failure in the Punjab had been more apparent than real. His patience and humility had won him many admirers, and dislike for his rivals grew steadily among the Sikhs. When Aurangzeb began a persecution of Sikhs the rival leaders melted away and messengers came to Tegh Bahadur asking him to become a shepherd to his people. The Guru immediately went to the aid of his people.

He discovered that the officials of Aurangzeb had been using a variety of methods to discourage the Hindu and Sikh religions and promote Islam. Temples had been destroyed, the Moslems regarding them as places of idolatry. Pilgrims had been discouraged by being forced to pay extra taxes. Tegh Bahadur encouraged Hindus and Sikhs to remain loyal to their beliefs and as he travelled through the Punjab crowds came to listen and went away determined to resist in order to preserve religious freedom.

Tegh Bahadur was arrested at Agra and taken under heavy guard to Delhi where he was brought before the Emperor's representative, for Aurangzeb was not in the city. The Guru was sentenced to death and was decapitated on November 11th, 1675. He had died as much for Hindu freedom as for Sikh, as his son

Gobind noted in some verses he wrote
about the martyrdom:

> 'To protect their right to wear their caste mark
>   and sacred threads
> Did he, in the dark age, perform the supreme
>   sacrifice.
> To help the saintly he went to the utmost limit,
> He gave his head but never cried in pain.'

THE TENTH GURU:
GOBIND SINGH (1666–1708)

Guru Gobind Rai became leader of the Sikhs at the
age of eleven. He decided that 'when all other
means have failed it is righteous to draw the sword'.
Therefore, he summoned the Sikhs to Anandpur
on the first day of the month Baisakhi 1699.

The story of what happened next is one of the
most famous in Sikh history, one which the Sikhs
never tire of telling. Mr. Ruprai was able to create
an atmosphere which no book can convey when he
told it to Kishan and Alan.

In uniform and fully armed the Guru stood before
his people, sword in hand.

"Today, I want the head of a Sikh", he said. "Who
will offer his life to his Guru?"

Not one of the many thousands who heard him
spoke. Three times the Guru repeated his demand
and the crowd became more and more afraid. Then
Daya Ram, a Kshatriya of Lahore, came forward.
"My head is at your service, my true Lord. There
can be no greater gain than to die under your
sword."

Gobind took him into a tent near by. After a few
minutes he returned, his sword dripping blood, and
repeated his demand. Dharam Dass, a Jat or

peasant from Delhi, offered himself and followed the Guru to the tent. Thrice more the guru asked for a victim; Muhkam Chand, a washerman from Dwarka, Himmat, a potter from Jagganath, and Sahib Chand, a barber from Bidar, all members of the servant caste, stepped forward in turn.

After the fifth had entered the tent Guru Gobind came to his followers again—this time not with a dripping sword but with the five men, unharmed.

He told the shocked but relieved audience that they must form themselves into a brotherhood, fearless and ready to give their lives for the faith. This brotherhood must be free from caste and therefore, he said, all its members should first drink together from the same bowl a mixture of sugar and water called **amrit** and then share the same surname of **Singh** (which means 'lion').

The first five members of this brotherhood called the **Khalsa,** or 'pure ones', were those who had offered their lives to the Guru. They are known among the Sikhs as the **Panj Pyare** (the Beloved Five). The sixth member was the Guru, who insisted on being baptised to show the equality of all men. His name now became Gobind Singh. 20,000 other Sikhs were baptised that day. Women members of the **Khalsa** took the name **Kaur** (Princess).

Each man took an oath to wear the hair long, never to have it cut, and never to shave his beard: to keep the hair in place with a comb: to wear a pair of shorts which would make movement easy in battle: to wear a steel bracelet on the right wrist and to carry a sword. They were given four rules, not to cut their hair, not to eat meat killed in Moslem fashion (by being bled to death), not to smoke or drink alcohol, and not to harm Moslem women—which might well happen during war.

In addition Sikh men were to wear the turban so that they could be clearly recognised as Sikhs.

Now no Hindu would come to harm by being
mistaken for a Sikh and no timid Sikh would be
able to pretend he was a Hindu. He would stand
up for his faith, he would fight to defend it— but
he would never force his beliefs upon anyone else.

THE INITIATION CEREMONY AND THE
MEANING OF THE '5 Ks'

Guru Gobind Singh intended the Khalsa to be a
permanent institution. One day Kishan and Pritam
would be initiated into it, but not until they were
old enough to understand the significance of
membership. The ceremony is as follows. **Amrit**,
the baptism nectar, is made in an iron bowl from
water sweetened by sugar and stirred by five Sikhs
with a **khanda** (a double-edged sword) passed from
one to another. The senior one of them reads the
famous poem of Guru Nanak called the **Japji** while
the others squat, their left knee on the ground,
their right knee raised ready to spring into action
should an enemy appear. After the **Japji**, a poem
the **Jap Sahib**, by Guru Gobind Singh, is read by
another Sikh, next in seniority. Each Sikh reads
while the **Amrit** is stirred and when the last has
read an evening prayer, the **Anand** (Song of Bliss),
the young man who is to be baptised squats like
the others (it is called sitting **Vir Asan**—in the
posture of the warrior). He recites, **Wahe Guru Ji
Ka Khalsa Sri Wahe Guru Ji Ki Fateh** (The
Khalsa is of God and the Victory is to God) while
the senior Sikh pours **Amrit** into his hands and
asks him to drink it. This is repeated five times.
Some **Amrit** is then sprinkled into his eyes; it is
thrown with some force but he should not blink.
After this the man's turban is moved slightly and
some **Amrit** placed on his head.

When all the candidates have been baptised the **Anand** is sung, prayer is offered and the service ends with everyone sharing the **Karah Parshad**.

The five Ks are worn by all baptised Sikhs:

1. The **Kesh**: the long uncut hair and unshaven beard. In many religions these symbolise complete devotion to God. Samson, John the Baptist and many other Jews, some Moslems and many Hindus showed their faithfulness to God in this way.
2. **Kanga**: the comb. This keeps the hair tidy and in place and so symbolises discipline.
3. **Kachs**: shorts. They enabled freedom of movement in battle and were much better for this reason than the Hindu **dhoti**. They symbolise spiritual freedom.
4. **Kara**: steel bracelet. It is worn on the right wrist. Once it protected the hand against the twanging of the bowstring but its spiritual symbolism lies in its roundness and the steel from which it is made. Steel symbolises strength, a Sikh cannot be broken under stress. As a ring is a symbol of unity, for example the unity between man and wife, the Sikh's **Kara** represents the unity of Sikhs in one brotherhood and reminds him of his allegiance to the **Khalsa**.
5. **Kirpan**: sword. This is the symbol of authority and justice and reminds the Sikh of his duty to defend the right and also that God is the defender of Truth.

The carrying of flick knives or daggers is forbidden under English law. They are regarded as offensive weapons. Many Sikhs in England do not wear a **kirpan**, others carry a very small one, not as big as a pen-knife.

THE TEN GURUS   53

Sometimes a very small symbolic **kirpan** is embedded in the wooden **kanga** the Sikh wears in his hair.

GURU GOBIND SINGH AND BHAI GHANAYA

Sadly, from the time of the formation of the Khalsa, wars with Moslems were frequent but the ideas of the brotherhood of all men taught by Guru Nanak were not forgotten.

During a battle between Moslems and Sikhs, a Sikh water carrier called Ghanaya was seen giving water to wounded Moslem soldiers as they lay suffering from thirst under the hot sun. He was brought to Guru Gobind Singh and accused of being a traitor. The Guru heard the charges and asked Ghanaya to answer them. "When I walked through the battlefields I saw no Moslems and no Sikhs, only your face in every man", said Ghanaya. "You are a true Sikh", replied the Guru. "Continue the work; and here is some ointment to put on the wounds. You shall be known as Bhai Ghanaya from now on!" (As we saw with Bhai Buddha, **bhai** means brother, but it is a term of honour among Sikhs, reserved for the best of men.)

The motto of the warrior Guru is said to have been 'Know that all mankind is one caste'. The story of Bhai Ghanaya shows that Guru Gobind Singh was more than a soldier.

GURU GOBIND SINGH: SPIRITUAL TEACHER

Gobind Singh was not only a soldier, he was also a spiritual leader of his people, their guru. He is often known as the soldier saint.

He taught that the end of man is union with God.
He described it in this way.

'As sparks flying out of a flame
Fall back on the fire from which they rise,
As dust rising from the earth
Falls back upon the same earth;
As waves beating upon the shingle
Recede and in the ocean mingle
So from God come all things under the sun
And to God return when their race is run.'

Guru Gobind Singh was a humble man and
realised that his followers might make too much of
him by giving him the worship men should give only
to God.

He wrote:
'Though my thoughts are lost in prayer
At the feet of Almighty God,
I was ordained to establish a sect and lay down
    its rules
But whoever regards me as Lord
Shall be damned and destroyed.'
'I am—and of this let there be no doubt—
I am but a slave of God as other men are,
A beholder of the wonders of creation.'

He was a busy man but did not neglect prayer
and meditation. God, he said, reveals Himself to
men, shows them His love, provides them with
wisdom through the teaching of the gurus, but He
is beyond human understanding:

'Some worship stones and on their heads they
    bear them.
Some behold the God in the south, some bow
    their head to the west,

Some worship images, others are busy praying
    to the dead,
The world is thus bound in false ritual
And God's secret is still unread.'

Guru Gobind Singh was also a poet but he
included none of his own hymns in the **Granth**.
After his death Bhai Mani Singh collected his
verses, some 2,000 in a number of languages
including Persian and Punjabi, and these formed
the **Dasam Granth**, the book of the Tenth Guru.

One of them praises his followers:

'All the battles I have won against tyranny
I have fought with the devoted backing of these
    people;
Through them only have I been able to bestow
    gifts,
Through their help I have escaped from harm;
The love and the generosity of these Sikhs
Have enriched my heart and my home.'
'Through their grace I have attained all learning;
Through their help in battle, I have slain all my
    enemies.
I was born to serve them, through them I reached
    eminence.
What would I have been without their kind and
    ready help?
There are millions of insignificant people like me.
True service is the service of these people:
I am not included to serve others of higher
castes;
Charity will bear fruit, in this and the next world,
If given to such worthy people as these.
All other sacrifices and charities are pointless.
From top to toe, whatever I call my own,
    All I possess or carry, I dedicate to these people.

In another verse he sums up Sikh teaching about God:

'He has no name, no dwelling-place, no caste;
He has no shape, or colour, or outer limits.
He is the Primal Being, Gracious and Benign,
Unborn, ever Perfect, and Eternal.
He is of no nation, and wears no distinguishing
    garb;
He has no outer likeness; He is free from desire.
To the east or to the west,
Look where you may,
He pervades and prevails
As Love and Affection.'

C   PROJECT WORK

*The story of the Sikhs is only one important part of
the history and religion of India.*

*There are a number of ways in which the Sikhs
might be put into their Indian and world context.*

1. *Make a large wall map showing the Punjab in
   relation to Pakistan and India.*
2. *Make a relief map of the Punjab showing the
   mountains and deserts which surround it and
   the rivers which flow through it.*
3. *Complete the time chart on the next page
   adding columns showing important events in
   Sikh history, which you can discover from this
   book and things which were happening in
   England at the same time.*

Europe	England	The Sikhs	India
			1451 Rule of Lodi kings begins in Delhi.
1453 Fall of Constantinople.			
		1469 Birth of Guru Nanak	
1492 Columbus lands in the Bahamas			
			1498 Arrival of Vasco Da Gama
1508 Michelangelo begins work in the Sistine Chapel			
1517 Luther's 95 theses			
			1526 Babur founds Mogul rule in Delhi.
			1556 Accession of Akbar
1564 Birth of Galileo (died 1643)			
1571 Battle of Lepanto			
1643 Reign of Louis XIV (to 1715)			
			1657 Accession of Aurangzeb
			1674 Maharatta rebellion against Moguls (led by Sivaji)
1685 Handel born (died 1759)			
1704 Battle of Blenheim			1707 Death of Aurangzeb
		1708 Death of Guru Gobind Singh	

THE TEN GURUS

THE GURU GRANTH SAHIB

Before taking Alan to the **Gurdwara** Mr. Ruprai said there was one further explanation he must give, and that was about the **Granth**.

He went to the bookshelf and took down two large volumes with hard red covers. Each was about a foot high, almost two inches thick and very heavy.

"This", he said "is the **Granth**, our holy book. In the Temple you will see it resting in the place of honour, upon a throne and under a canopy. This two-volume edition was quite expensive. If you wanted to buy an English translation you would have to pay about £14."

He reminded Alan how Guru Angad had instructed the hymns of Guru Nanak to be written down, and how, when the Golden Temple was built a copy was installed in it.

He also told him that Guru Arjan selected hymns composed by Hindus and Moslems as well as Sikhs, and Bhai Gurdas copied them into the book.

This is a remarkable feature of the **Granth**. Few if any other scriptures contain passages written by men of a different faith. There are almost 1,000 poems by non-Sikhs in the **Adi Granth**.

Sheikh Farid was a Moslem, a nephew of a thirteenth century king of Ghazni. He wrote 134 poems in Punjabi which Guru Nanak obtained.

'Farid, should any man smite thee
Return not blow for blow,
Nay kiss his feet that smiteth thee
And go peacefully homeward.

Farid, return good for evil,
Let not the sun go down upon thy wrath,
Thy body shall be free from sorrowing,
All things thou most desirest thou shalt have.'

THE GRANTH

Apparently the monsoons could not prevent
Farid worshipping in the mosque. He let nothing
stand between him and God:

'Let the rains come down in torrents, Lord,
And pelt and drench my garments,
Yet I go to meet the Beloved Friend
Lest I break the ties of love.'

Other Moslems with hymns in the **Granth** include
Mardana, Nanak's close friend and disciple, the
professional musician and folk singer.

Kabir, the famous fifteenth century Indian poet, is
claimed by both Moslems and Hindus and 541 of
his hymns are in the **Adi Granth**. Like Nanak he
was critical of Hinduism and Islam and looked for
the truth of God in the heart:

'Kabir, why, O Mullah, do you climb up to your
    minaret?
Do you think the Lord is hard of hearing?
Seek in your heart for Him for whose sake
You call so loudly to prayer!'

A tailor, a cobbler, a court barber and Sadhana,
a butcher, who used to weigh the meat he sold
with an idol to show his disgust with idol worship,
are among Hindus whose writings are included.
Sadhana is said to have been put to death for his
beliefs in the thirteenth century by a Sultan who
had him bricked up alive. There is a poem by a
Brahmin, Parmanand, as well as by low-caste and
untouchable Hindus.

Although most of the 5,894 hymns are in Punjabi,
some are in medieval Hindi.

The biggest contribution is from Guru Arjan,
2,216 hymns. His most famous poem is **Sukhmani**,
the Hymn of Peace. Its teaching is that the health

and peace of the soul comes from continually
calling to mind the name of God.

This is one of his verses:

'Of all Religions this is the best Religion,
To utter the Holy Name with adoration, and to do
    great deeds:
Of all rites the holiest rite
Is to cleanse one's soul in the company of the
    saints:
Of all strivings the best striving
To meditate on the Name and praise it for ever:
Of all speeches, the ambrosial speech is
To utter aloud, having hearkened to it, God's
    glory:
Of all shrines, the most sacred shrine,
Nanak, is the heart in which the Lord dwells.'

It ends:

'He in whose heart this Song of Peace dwells,
Or he who hears it with loving heart
In him the Lord's remembrance is awakened,
The pangs of death and the new birth are
    destroyed,
His precious soul forthwith attains salvation;
His flame shall be spotless and his speech like
    nectar;
The name of God shall now pervade his soul.
Sorrow and sickness, fear and doubt will vanish.
His acts shall be pure: men will call him a saint,
And his life shall be blessed with the highest
    glory,
Nanak saith: Because of these virtues
This is called Sukhmani, the hymn of peace.'

Sometimes the **Granth** is called the **Adi Granth**
which means 'first word'. This distinguishes it from

Dasam Granth or book of the tenth Guru which is referred to at the end of this section.

The **Granth** was finalised by Guru Gobind Singh in 1706. His friend Bhai Mani Singh acted as scribe.

Before his death the tenth Guru chose no human successor, as the nine previous gurus had done, but said that the **Granth** would be the permanent Guru. Sikhs therefore treat it with great respect and usually call it the **Guru Granth Sahib**.

'Sahib' is a term something like 'Sir'. It may seem odd to use it when speaking of a book but then the book is a living voice, not a dead letter. Through the **Granth** God speaks to men as he spoke to them through Nanak, Angad and the other teachers.

In worship it is treated with the utmost reverence. Its pages are not touched with unwashed hands, and when it is carried into a room everyone stands and bows towards it. In the hall where the services are held, as we have seen, it is given the one place of honour, upon the dais, and everyone kneels in front of it before sitting down. The correct name fo the dais is **takht,** which means throne. The **Guru Granth Sahib** is enthroned as the later Gurus wer A man sits behind it with a **chauri** (not a fly whisk, but a sign of authority, such as that carried by the African leader Jomo Kenyatta) just as he would have stood by Guru Gobind Singh nearly three hundred years ago. When it is not being read it is covered. It may be read by anyone, man or woman. The reader is called the **Granthi**.

Sikhs believe that the **Granth** is their guide throughout life in everything they do. They believe that its teachings will only be respected if the book is treated with reverence.

The **Granth** is the Guru of the Sikhs. In its presence they are named, baptised, and married. It is the centre of their worship and their lives.

THE SIKH LANGUAGE

The Sikh language, Punjabi, is written from left to right. Altogether it has 35 characters and these are some of them, with their English equivalents.

a	b	ch	d	e	f	g	h
ਅ	ਬ	ਚ	ਡ	ਏ	ਫ	ਗ	ਹ

j	k	kh	l	m	n	ng	o
ਜ	ਕ	ਖ	ਲ	ਮ	ਨ	ਙ	ਓ

p	r	s	sh	t	th	v	y
ਪ	ਰ	ਸ	ਸ਼	ਟ	ਠ	ਵ	ਯ

These are some common words in Punjabi:

man	woman	boy	girl	guru	Nanak
ਆਦਮੀ	ਤੀਂਵੀਂ	ਮੁੰਡਾ	ਕੁੜੀ	ਗੁਰੂ	ਨਾਨਕ

This is the Mool Mantra, the basic mantra or teaching of the Sikhs. It is printed in Punjabi with the English transliteration beneath each word:

੧ ਓ ਸਤਿਨਾਮ	ਕਰਤਾ	ਪੁਰਖੁ	ਨਿਰਭਉ	ਨਿਰਵੈਰੁ
Ek onkar satnam	karta	purkh	nirbau	nirvair

ਅਕਾਲਮੂਰਤਿ	ਅਜੂਨੀ	ਸੈਭੰ	ਗੁਰਪ੍ਰਸਾਦਿ ॥
akalmurt	ajoni	saibhang	gurparsad

Here is the English translation:

There is One God,
He is the Supreme Truth
He, the Creator, is without fear
And without hate.

He, the Omnipresent, pervades the Universe,
He is not born, nor does He die to be born again.
By the grace of the Guru, the Enlightener,
True in the beginning, true throughout the ages,
True even now, and forever shall be true.

*You might like to compare Punjabi with Hindi, the Indian
language which you can see on postage stamps or on page
88 of "A Hindu Family in Britain" by Peter Bridger (Religious
Education Press). For further information, see "Teach Yourself Punjabi" by C. Shackle (English Universities Press).*

8 **A VISIT TO A SIKH TEMPLE**

One Sunday morning at 11.30 a.m. Mr. Ruprai's car stopped outside Alan's house. Alan was ready and waiting to go to the Sikh Temple. Normally on Sunday he didn't wear his cap but this morning he had put it on because Kishan had told him that in the Temple people cover their heads and take off their shoes.

Kishan explained that usually they went to the Temple before ten o'clock but as the service was in Punjabi and Alan wouldn't understand it they had decided to go later this week so that he wouldn't be bored.

They reached the Temple, or **Gurdwara** as Kishan called it, and parked the car. Pritam Kaur and her mother went in at the door on the left. Mr. Ruprai and Kishan, with Alan, used the right-hand entrance.

Inside the porch was a counter and behind it racks. The boys and Mr. Ruprai gave their shoes to a man who put them on the rack and gave Mr. Ruprai a metal disc with a number on it. On the other side, though Alan couldn't see it, the same thing was happening. Then Mrs. Ruprai and Pritam pulled their **dupattas** (silk shoulder-scarves) over their heads and opened the door into the Temple. By this time Mr. Ruprai and the boys were already sitting cross-legged on the floor at the other side of the hall. Mrs. Ruprai and her daughter placed some money on a cloth which already had a pile of money on it and bowed low in front of the dais. They then sat down among the other women. About 300 people were in the room.

It was as though Alan had entered another world. The only things which seemed familiar to him were the suits which the men were wearing, just like his father's, and the decorations. There were streamers and fairy lights as though the room were decorated for Christmas. These and the beautiful bright clothes of the women and the turbans of the men,

with the cream-coloured walls made everything very joyful. The small children, boys as well as girls, were with their mothers. Sometimes they would stand up, and occasionally move quietly to another group of children; one little boy went across to his father and after a few minutes returned to his sisters and mother. How unlike Alan's own church it was.

When he had grown accustomed to the colourful scene he looked more attentively at the platform. In the centre was a canopy with strangely written words on the front. Under the canopy a man was sitting cross-legged behind a cloth-covered dais. He was occasionally waving something in a slow dignified way. Later Kishan told him this was a **chauri**. It was made of silver and had animal hairs fastened into one end. Mr. Ruprai said it was a sign of authority, something like a sceptre.

To one side of the dais, on the platform were three musicians playing a **sitar**, a harmonium and a drum which Kishan called a **tabla** or **jori**. One was singing into a microphone. The congregation was listening.

When the music stopped the singer spoke for about ten minutes. Alan supposed it was a sermon. He heard the words **'Nanak'** and **'Khalsa'** spoken frequently and sometimes it seemed as though the man were reciting poetry.

The singing began again without musical accompaniment. Everyone stood facing the platform.

Occasionally everyone said **'waheguru'**, as a response, while one man said a prayer called **Ardas** and at the end of it **'waheguru ji ka khalsa, waheguru ji ki fateh** very loudly. This means 'The Sikhs are chosen of God, to God be the victory!'

A VISIT TO A SIKH TEMPLE

The service ended with someone shouting **'Jo bole so nihal'**, a warcry which defies translation, and everyone replying **'Sat sri-akal'**. Then everyone sat down.

Alan had noticed, during the hymns, that a man had stepped on to the platform and had taken the covers from a large metal bowl which he hadn't seen before. He had taken his dagger and put it into the bowl. Now something was spooned from the bowl into others, and a number of the men and women began walking among the seated worshippers giving everyone a handful.

"It's the **Parshad**", said Kishan.

"**Parshad**?" echoed Alan. "That's right", said Kishan. "It's made of equal parts of flour, melted butter, water and sugar." By that time one of the men had reached Alan. He stooped down and put a small helping of **Parshad**, about the size of a golf ball, into his hands. Holding it in his left hand Alan gingerly put some of the warm, sticky food into his mouth with his right hand. "Hmm. Not bad," he said, putting the rest into his mouth, then he wiped his hands.

By now everyone was standing up and talking in groups. Pritam Kaur came over to join her brother and Alan, and they took him to meet Mr. Virdi, the president of the **Gurdwara**.

"**Sat sri akal**" he said. "How do you do? Did you understand much of our service?"

"Not really", said Alan. "But I think I got some idea of what it all meant, even if I couldn't understand the words. We all sat on the floor facing the platform and no one was dressed differently and no one sat in a special place. That means that everyone is equal. I suppose the **Parshad**, which we all

shared, meant the same thing." "Very good"
said Mr. Virdi. "You're perfectly right. That the men
and women didn't sit together meant nothing, it's
just a custom. We ate together and that is what
matters. Also, as you saw, members of the congregation did everything. We have no ministers or
priests."

"One thing I didn't understand was the man with
the **chauri**", confessed Alan. "Then come with
me", replied Mr. Virdi, "and we will see if we can
explain." He led Alan, Pritam Kaur and Kishan
on to the platform and round the back of the dais.
He lifted back a beautiful pink cloth revealing a
large book. "This", he said "is the **Granth**, our
Holy Book written in a script used four hundred
years ago. It contains our religious teaching. We
treat it with great respect, as one would honour a
great king. It has the chief place in our **Gurdwara**,
high above anyone else. A man sits behind it,
waving the **chauri**, a symbol of authority, over it
whenever it is open."

It was now time to go home. "Goodbye, Alan,
come again soon, then we can show you the guest
room and the kitchen." Turning to Pritam and
Kishan, Mr. Virdi continued, "Goodbye, Pritam
Kaur, goodbye, Kishan Singh."

As they went to the car Kishan told Alan that
Mr. Virdi always addressed them as Pritam Kaur
and Kishan Singh. It was to teach them self-respect
—that they were a princess and a lion, he explained—
and to remind them that they were Sikhs.

D PROJECT WORK

1. *In the **Granth** it is written 'Let no one be proud of his caste . . . . the world is made of one clay'. Find out how the caste system works. See "A Hindu Family in Britain", by Peter Bridger, another book in this series, chapter 11. How do Sikhs show that they do not believe in caste?*
2. *The Sikhs call their meeting for worship **Diwan**. In the India of Nanak's day a **Diwan** was the assembly of the Emperor when he gave his people an audience. Can you see how the Sikh worship resembles the **Diwan** of an Emperor?*

Try to visit a **Gurdwara** one Sunday morning. Write to the secretary to make arrangements. You will find him most helpful and you will be made very welcome.

It may be possible to tape-record part of the service and the president may permit someone to take a few photographs when the service has ended.

Back at school you can sketch from memory or paint pictures of the **granthi** or **takht**, the musicians and the beautiful clothes worn by the ladies.

An exhibition arising from your study and visit could be mounted in the hall to provide background to an act of worship using Sikh readings and prayers.

Some of the places where there is a **Gurdwara:**

Birmingham	Leeds
Bradford	Leicester
Bristol	London
Cardiff	Manchester
Coventry	Newcastle upon Tyne
Derby	Nottingham
Doncaster	Portsmouth
Glasgow	Slough
Gravesend	Southampton
Huddersfield	Wolverhampton
Leamington Spa	

In a number of large cities there is more than one **Gurdwara**. Often they are houses, churches or business premises which have been converted. A number of purpose-built **Gurdwaras** are now under construction.

At the back of the book is a short list of addresses. By writing to one of them you will be able to obtain the precise address of the **Gurdwara** you wish to visit and probably the name of the secretary to whom you should write.

SIKH NAMES The birth of a baby into a happy home is always a wonderful event. All the relatives are informed and presents are given.

Hindus often put a little mark of soot or some dark paste on the baby, perhaps behind an ear or on the forehead so that visitors will not comment too enthusiastically upon the beauty of the baby, and so perhaps bring misfortune upon it.

Sikhs have no such beliefs and fears. Visitors to the house are shown the baby and given tea and sweets. They often bring gifts of baby clothes or money.

It is a costly as well as a happy occasion for the parents. While this book was being written a little boy, Jaswant, was born into the home of a Sikh friend. This was the first boy for 36 years in the family and naturally everyone was overjoyed. The father spent a week taking gifts to relatives and friends—a new **shalwar, kameeze** and **dupatta** to women relatives, a turban and shirt to men, a bag of sweets to friends. These are traditional Sikh gifts and must have cost the family well over £100.

Sweets are to be found on many occasions, sometimes given out after the **Karah Parshad** at a service, always on the table at a wedding. They are made of gram flour, sugar and clarified butter. How they are made will be described at the end of this section.

When a baby has been born into a Sikh home, and as soon as the mother is well enough to go to the **Gurdwara,** the baby is presented before the **Guru Granth Sahib. Amrit** is prepared from water and sugar and five verses of the **Japji** are recited.

A prayer is offered, called the **Ardas**. Part of it says:

'Every day is a day gone
Out of thy life,
Search out the knower of God
And improve thy life.

This world is drowning in a sea of doubt
Only the knower of God walks across it.
Whomsoever He awakens, and gives a taste of
this nectar,
He only knows that which cannot be told.

Know the real purpose of thy being here and
gather up the treasure,
Under the guidance of the true Teacher
Make thy mind the dwelling-place of God.'

The prayer ends with these words:

'I present this child and with Thy grace I
administer him the **Amrit**.
May he be a true Sikh,
May he devote himself to the service of his
fellowmen and his motherland.
May he be inspired with devotion,
May the Holy Food be acceptable (to the Guru)
By the ever-increasing glory of thy Name;
May the whole creation be blessed.'

Amrit is dropped into the baby's mouth, the
mother drinks the rest and the **Granth** is opened
at random. The first letter of the first hymn on the
page is declared to be the initial of the child's
name. So with Kishan Ruprai the first letter was
'K', with Pritam, his sister, 'P'.
The naming ceremony ends with everyone sharing
the **Karah Parshad**.
Names today are often given for family reasons
or simply because the parents like a certain name.
Once patriotic names were sometimes given like

Delhi-Tor-Singh (the Lion who will break Delhi), or military names like Jarnail, Karnail or Kaptan (General, Colonel, or Captain). Occasionally in England one hears of such names as Mafeking Williams or Trafalgar Brown or Marshall Hall, but nowadays both Sikhs and Englishmen tend to choose names without considering their meaning.

The study of British surnames can be fascinating. They can help us to find out where our ancestors came from long ago or discover what jobs they did. We all know that Jones and Price belong to Wales and McKenzie and Macpherson to Scotland. Miller, Archer and Cartwright tell us about the work members of our family did long ago. Hindu names were often descriptive of the caste to which people belonged. Because Sikhs disapproved of caste distinctions they tended to drop surnames and call all women **Kaur** (princess) and all men **Singh** (lion) as terms of respect. Some names, however, are very common, and to distinguish one person from another nicknames or village names were added and these became surnames, for example, Dalip Singh Ainki (one who wears glasses) or Dalip Singh Bhakna (who comes from the village of Bhakna)—rather like 'Jones-the-bread' or 'Jones-one-leg' in Wales.

In some English schools there may be a number of Sikhs in one class. There is enough confusion with two or three 'Smiths', so in school Kishan Singh is called Kishan Singh Ruprai and his sister Pritam Kaur Ruprai. **'Kaur'** and **'Singh'** must never be separated from the first name.

A further complication arises from the fact that some names, such as Pritam and Jaswant, may belong to men or women.

10 **SIKH FOODS** One of the most important arts for anyone to learn is that of cooking. Home economics (or domestic science) courses in schools sometimes attract boys as well as girls, dozens of recipe books are published each year and television programmes on cookery are always popular. Against this there is the problem of time. Life is such a rush that the range of 'instant' foods increases almost weekly. Grandmother probably baked her own bread and was proud of her home-made Christmas cakes and Christmas puddings. Nowadays it is possible to feed on frozen or tinned foods from breakfast to supper and many people do.

In India life is far less hurried and Indians now living in Britain still enjoy preparing a meal for visitors. Mothers very carefully teach their daughters cookery, for an Indian wife is expected to feed her family well and to be an expert cook.

Often, as in an English home, everyone is at work during the day, including mother. The children may have had school lunches, father and mother may have taken sandwiches or soup or had a meal in the canteen at lunch time. In the evening the family gathers together. Now is the time for them to enjoy a leisurely meal. This can be a far greater delight than going to the cinema or to the theatre. The mother or the daughters have been able to show their skills as cooks and everyone can eat and talk in peace and without hurry.

Sikhs may eat any meat. Unlike the Hindus they may eat beef and they are not vegetarians. The Ruprias simply observe one food regulation, namely that the animal must not have been killed according to Moslem custom, that is by having an artery in the throat cut. There seem to be two reasons for this objection. First they consider the method cruel (Moslems disagree strongly), and secondly, sometimes Hindus accused Sikhs of being Moslem converts. By eating beef, but not if it had been slaughtered by Moslems, the Sikhs showed that they were a distinct group—neither Moslem nor Hindu. Because Sikhs have always lived among Hindus they frequently do not eat beef—out of consideration for Hindu feelings.

Though they are not vegetarians the Ruprais often enjoy tasty vegetarian meals. In the hot sunny climate of India meat is not regarded as an essential part of the diet and is often very expensive. In Britain the Ruprais continue to enjoy their Indian foods—though Kishan and Pritam are also very fond of fish and chips!

One simple food which Mrs. Ruprai knows always pleases her family is **Pakora**. A batter is made from gram flour (made from lentils or peas) and water, to which are added a number of spices, salt and pepper. Depending upon the palates of the guests the mixture can be keenly or moderately spiced. Mrs. Ruprai leaves out the hottest chillies when she has English visitors. Mrs. Ruprai thinly slices some potatoes, if the dish is to be potato pakora, dips each piece into the batter and then drops it into a pan of hot ghee or vegetable oil to fry until brown. Instead of potatoes, cauliflower, tomatoes, sliced onions or fish can be used. The fritters are eaten with the fingers and may be served hot or warm. They are crisp and only slightly greasy.

The **Chapatti** is probably the best-known Indian food. Mr. Bridger (A Hindu Family in Britain, p. 66) has described one method of preparing it but some Indians use others and there is more than one sort of chapatti. One is **Tandori Riote** made of brown flour and water which is mixed into a thick batter, and the chapatti which results is about half an inch thick. Water or ghee is spread thinly on one side of it and it is put into a pan of warm fat, water side down. After a few minutes it is taken out of the pan and baked in the oven like a cake.

Prawnta is a chapatti with a butter filling. This is fried on a hotplate with margarine or ghee. Prawnta can also have a filling of mince, mashed potatoes or cauliflower.

Puria is a type of chapatti in which the water-flour mixture is a firmer one, and the chapatti is deep fried.

Pappadoms are an Indian dish becoming popular among English people. These are difficult to make and many Sikh housewives buy them ready made from an Indian shop and fry them for two or three minutes in hot, but not boiling vegetable oil. The result is a wafer-thin crisp savoury.

Tandori Chicken is very popular with the Ruprai family. A batter is made which has plain yoghourt as its base. To this may be added pepper, salt, powdered or grated garlic, ginger and other spices according to taste. Small pieces of chicken are dipped into this and then placed on a plate to allow the batter to soak in. When the family is ready for the meal the meat is grilled or roasted in silver foil coated with ghee to prevent it sticking. The dish is decorated with pieces of lemon or tomato.

Besides savouries Indians also enjoy sweets and often these are served as the sweet course of a meal.

Though Indian sweets have many names and various shapes the main ingredients seem to be gram flour, sugar and ghee (clarified butter).

Jalebis differ in shape. They look like thin barley sugar sticks twisted into figures of eight and similar shapes but to a European palate the different varieties taste much the same.

It was a sweet called **Lado** (pronounced Ladoo) that Alan saw being prepared.

The Sikh confectioner told him that the ingredients were gram flour and sugar in the proportion 2 lbs. of sugar to 1 lb. of flour. Colouring matter made them yellow-orange.

Alan saw three vats in the room where the sweets were made. In the first, nearest the door to the shop, was a batter of gram flour and water. It looked rather like pancake batter. Another pan contained hot sugar and water, kept on the boil.

The middle vat was two-thirds full of boiling ghee, bubbling like oil in a massive chip pan. Now and again Mr. Sidhu skimmed the surface to remove any scum which might form.

"Stand back now", he said, and with a ladle which had a number of small holes in it, scooped up some batter and held it over the boiling oil. The oil hissed and leaped angrily as the batter fell into it. Alan, who was already eight feet away, moved back involuntarily another yard. He now knew why Mr. Sidhu was the first Sikh he had met who wore heavy boots!

In less than a minute, or so it seemed, the cooked batter had risen to the surface. Mr. Sidhu skimmed it off, let the hot oil drip from it. The batter had been baked into orange flakes which he now threw into another larger vat containing the hot sugar and water mixture. Now and again more mixture was added from the constantly boiling vat of sugar and water to soak into the steadily increasing pile of flakes so as to sweeten them.

After soaking it was strained and the flakes, now sticking together, were put in another long pan to cool. Mr. Sidhu's son moulded it into orange balls about the size of table tennis balls.

The sweets sell at about twenty or twenty-five new pence a pound and you do not get many **Lado** to the pound, but when Alan had eaten just two he felt full. The sugar, flour and butter produced something much richer and sweeter than fudge or any other sweet he had tasted.

11 A SIKH WEDDING

Weddings are gay and happy affairs all over the world and in every religion. Presents are given, families gather together, rice or confetti is thrown, and there are wonderful displays of flowers to provide colour and scent.

A Sikh wedding is no exception, as Alan discovered when he went with his parents, at the invitation of Mr. and Mrs. Ruprai, to the wedding of a niece of theirs, Kalwant Kaur.

Getting married is not simply an event lasting an hour. There are many things to be done before the day. Invitations have to be sent, the reception planned, clothes bought and the day fixed or confirmed with the minister or registry office. Sikhs have no ministers but they need to arrange with the **Gurdwara** committee to avoid clashing with other couples or other festivities.

We consider marriage to be a private matter between two individuals marrying for love. This is how Europeans think; but not Hindus, Pakistanis, Sikhs and many other people from Asia or Africa. In these communities a marriage concerns two whole families, not just two people, and it demands much careful thought. The families must not be related and in villages often they are. Hindus of different castes should not marry one another. They must have similar interests and not be hostile to one another. If the two fathers are competitors in business it is unlikely that they will be able to co-operate in helping their children make a success of marriage.

Arranged marriages used to be fairly common in Britain among the nobility or in wealthy business families. Coming-out parties and balls were a popular method employed by parents to enable their children to meet suitable young gentlemen or ladies. While the couples were dancing, their parents were discussing ways and means for guiding them in the approved direction to the right partner.

When Mr. and Mrs. Ruprai were married they had only met once before the wedding, for a few hours at a party, and they had never been alone together. When Mr. Ruprai was in his early twenties his father told his brothers, a cousin and a few uncles that his son was ready to marry. One of them had a friend with a twenty-year-old daughter. After each family had found out what they could about the other a meeting was arranged and Mr. Ruprai and his son went to the girl's home. On this occasion the two who were to be married did not see one another. However, the girl's father clearly approved of the young man and a party was arranged at which the couple could meet.

The wedding took place a month later.

The marriage of Kalwant Kaur, Mr. Ruprai's niece, to Rajvir Singh was the one to which the Clark family was invited. Kalwant had lived in Britain for seven years, had gone to an English secondary school and worked as a typist. She had seen Rajvir at the **Gurdwara** and when her mother asked her about marriage she had told her that Rajvir was the sort of young man for her. He was good looking, he had many friends, he seemed kind. Kalwant knew his sister and even she thought her brother was a reasonable young man! The families met and agreed that Kalwant and Rajvir seemed suited to one another. The young couple decided to get to know one another before becoming betrothed. They went for walks, met at parties and visited one another's homes. At last they became engaged.

Everyone was happy. The families had been consulted and played their traditional part. Although they agreed it was good for the young people to get to know one another before marriage

A SIKH WEDDING

they could not go all the way with western ideas. The number of divorces in Britain made them suspicious of love-marriages. The young people were happy. They had been allowed their say and had been permitted to meet and become friends.

This was not marriage western-style. It was not marriage Indian-style. It was something different, and for Kalwant Kaur and Rajvir Singh it seemed a combination of the best of both worlds.

The betrothal or engagement was traditional and took place at Rajvir's home. Prayers were said in the front room in the presence of the **Guru Granth Sahib**. Kalwant's uncle took some dried fruit and a coconut and put them into a muslin scarf which Rajvir was carrying. Rajvir's parents sent Kalwant a ring and his parents gave her a suit of a **kameeze** or **shalwar**. Rajvir received a turban. The girl was not present at the betrothal.

Preparations for the wedding were made, invitations sent out and at last the day arrived.

The families assembled in their own homes and when Rajvir left for the **Gurdwara** he was given a tremendous send-off. His little sisters and nieces hugged him and giggled. His mother gave him another coconut to put in his scarf. She and the other women did not go to the service.

At the **Gurdwara** the male relatives of the bride and groom met in the **Langar**. They drank tea together and had a few biscuits and cakes to eat. A few senior members of Kalwant's family, an uncle and a brother, gave turbans to their opposite numbers in Rajvir's family. This coming together was called **Milani** which means 'meeting'.

A SIKH WEDDING

The menfolk then went into the hall where the service was to take place and sat down. As the day was a Sunday there were already many people present and the usual service was in progress. The groom sat in the congregation looking no different from anyone else except for his smart new turban which had a plume in it and the scarf which he held in his hand.

After about ten minutes things began to happen. The groom's father took a garland of flowers and put it round his son's shoulders. He took another and put it on the **Granth**. A few moments later someone beckoned to Rajvir who took his place on the platform in front of the **Granth**, sitting cross-legged. Some musicians who were friends of the groom replaced the others. They sang a few songs in his praise, which they had composed specially for the occasion and then sang a few hymns from the **Granth** about the sacredness of marriage and in which one of the Gurus stated that the best and happiest state of man is the married state.

While this was happening all eyes turned to the door. The bride came in dressed from head to foot in a deep red **dupatta, shalwar** and **kameeze** embroidered in gold. Her face was hidden by the **dupatta** pulled down over it, just as some western brides wear a veil when they get married. Another young woman, dressed almost like the bride, except that her **dupatta** did not veil her face, accompanied the bride. Mr. Ruprai said it was her sister though it could have been any female friend or relative of the bride. Both sat on the platform, Kalwant Kaur next to Rajvir Singh and her sister on her left with her arm round her.

One of the musicians began to speak. "Amongst us", he said, "marriage is not a social contract but aims at the fusion of two souls into one. It is a union on the long road of life."

A SIKH WEDDING

"Do you agree to accept the duties of marriage?" he asked. When the couple had bowed before the **Granth** to show that they did, the bride's father placed a garland of flowers on the **Granth** and one round the neck of both bride and groom. He then took Rajvir's saffron scarf—the one containing the coconuts and dried fruit and fastened it on to Kalwant Kaur's **dupatta**. By this act he publicly showed that he was giving his daughter to be Rajvir's wife.

After the marriage vows a hymn was read on behalf of the bride:

'Praise and blame I forsake both,
I seize the edge of your garment.
All else I let pass.
All relationships I found false.
I cling to Thee, my Lord.'

The most important part of the wedding is when the groom leads the bride four times round the **Granth**.

In an Indian wedding the couple walk round the sacred fire seven times but for the Sikhs the sacred book has taken the place of the sacred fire and the number has been reduced from seven to four.

Guru **Ram Das** composed a special hymn called **Lavan** (which means 'going round') to be sung at this stage of the service. It has four sections. While the couple are still seated the **Granthi** reads the first section and then it is sung by the musicians as the couple walk round the **Granth**:

'In the first round, the Lord ordains for you a
    secular life.
Accept the Guru's word as your scripture
And it will free you from sin.

Let your law of life be to meditate on the Name
 of God
Which is the theme of all scriptures.
Contemplate the true Guru, the perfect Guru
And all your sins shall depart.
Fortunate are those who hold God in their
 hearts;
They are ever serene and happy.
The slave Nanak declares that in the first round,
The marriage rite has begun.'

Each part of the **Lavan** tells the couple where the
source of true happiness lies, in devotion to God.
  With the fourth journey round the **Granth** the
Anand Karaj (ceremony of Bliss), as the wedding
service is called, is completed.
  As with all Sikh services, **Anand** is sung, the
prayer **Ardas** is said and everyone shares the
Karah Parshad; but before these there is a break
in the service.
  At the wedding of Kalwant and Rajvir, after the
fourth **Lavan,** Kalwant's mother came forward to
the seated couple. She carried some sweetmeats
in a small dish and put some in the mouth of her
son-in-law and gave some to her daughter. This
was her way of welcoming the young man into her
home and wishing both of them joy. Kalwant Kaur's
grandmother edged her way through the seated
womenfolk and put a garland round the necks of
the newlyweds. She also gave Rajvir Singh a
coconut.
  Alan could suppress his curiosity no longer—
"That's the third," he said, "Why?"
  "It may not be the last," replied Kishan. "The
coconut is to us what the horseshoe is to you.
Horseshoes are pretty odd things to give a bride
if you really think about it!"

A few other relatives garlanded the couple or brought tokens of affection to them. The musicians sang a further group of songs including one which they had composed as a wedding gift. **Anand, Ardas**, and the sharing of the **Karah Parshad** followed.

Only now did the newly married couple leave.

The reception took place in a restaurant. There was a fine variety of Indian dishes including many curries which Alan found very hot. He drank more fruit squash that afternoon than he had done for a long time! As the Sikhs are not vegetarian, meat was served in a number of different ways.

It was evening before Kalwant Kaur left for the home of Rajvir Singh, where she would live until they could buy a house of their own.

HOME LIFE When the newly married Kalwant and Rajvir set out from Kalwant's home, Alan noticed two things that were significant. First, Kalwant followed Rajvir down the path and into the waiting car. Secondly, it was with Rajvir's family that they would live, not with Kalwant's.

It is the duty of the Sikh wife to obey her husband, to follow him wherever he goes. It is the duty of the husband to provide his wife with a home.

The Sikh is a family man. One of the ideals put before young men and women is that of being married and bringing up a family. Marriage is the fulfilment of life, especially if the couple are blessed by having a son.

Even when Kalwant and Rajvir have their own home their parents will expect frequent visits from them and hope that they will settle down not far from Rajvir's family. Sikh parents take their responsibility for their children very seriously even when they are grown up and married. When they are younger should they wish to go out in the evenings their parents will expect to be told where they are going and who will be with them, and they will tell them to be home at a certain time. Parents also have a considerable say in the clothes boys and girls may wear.

The children recognise that their parents love them and that everything is done for their good. They respect their parents and obey them.

Girls in particular are expected to spend their evenings at home. They have so much to learn if they are to become good wives. They must learn how to cook a variety of dishes, both savouries and sweets. It is not enough to provide beans (from a tin) on toast! Also girls should know how to sew and embroider. In short, much of a daughter's life is devoted to learning how to become a wife and mother. Sikh mothers believe that the responsibility for educating their daughters in home-craft is theirs and should not be left to the school.

E THINGS TO DO

Write down as many reasons as you can in favour of arranged marriages.
Then:

Pretend you are a Sikh. Write a letter to an English friend explaining why you agree with arranged marriages.

Or:

Hold a class debate 'Marriage is far too serious to be left in the hands of two people'.

Try to find out what forms weddings take elsewhere in the world. Compare a Hindu and a Sikh wedding. See 'A Hindu Family in Britain', Chapter 5.
Do you agree that marriage is something sacred, not merely a social contract?

The **Granth** *says about women 'O man, why do you call her inferior? She is the mother of all great men, great rulers and great heroes.' How do Sikhs show respect for women?*

What do other religions teach about the equality of men and women?

Are men and women equal in Britain? Should they be?

Guru Ram Das said:

'They are not wife and husband who only sit
    together;
Rather are they wife and husband who have one
    spirit in two bodies.'

What do you think he meant?

Why do you think Sikhs disapprove of mixed marriages, that is a marriage between two people of different faiths?

13 **SIKH DRESS** At her wedding Kalwant Kaur wore the traditional costume of a Sikh woman.

Typical Indian dress is the **sari** made of one piece of material many yards long and wound carefully round the body.

Sikh women wear a tunic or frock called a **kameeze** which is a little longer than a mini skirt, and **shalwar (salwar)**, a form of trouser.

The **kameeze** fastens right up to the neck and has short sleeves, to the elbow. Kalwant's was almost knee-length and had a hem beautifully embroidered in gold.

The **shalwar** was loose fitting, gathered in at the ankles. Many of her friends were wearing **shalwar** which fitted more tightly to the leg, rather like jeans, but made of silk, nylon or cotton.

A Sikh woman wears a **dupatta** over her head. It is usually made of cotton and is either white or of some colour which will match the **kameeze**. Deep red is the traditional colour of a bride's clothes in India, whether she be Hindu, Moslem or Sikh. Kalwant Kaur wore red **dupatta, kameeze** and **shalwar**. The **shalwar** and **dupatta**, like the **kameeze**, were edged in gold thread.

The distinguishing feature of a Sikh man is his turban which may be of any colour—normally white or some shade of red, blue or green. The colour is not significant.

In the Punjab countryside a man will wear shorts (**kachs**) and a shirt or tunic hanging loosely outside them. In the town he will often wear western-style clothes as he does in Britain.

The **Turban** is not merely an article of dress. It is worn to keep the long hair (**kesh**) tidy but the comb (**kanga**) also does this. The most important reason for wearing the turban lies in the teaching of Guru Gobind Singh, founder of the **Khalsa**. He is reported to have said 'The **Khalsa** is in my

image and I reside in the **Khalsa'**, and to have told his followers that they should be moulded completely in his image. This, the **Khalsa** believed, meant that not only should they possess his faith and his courage but they should also dress like him, wearing the 'five Ks' and a turban. The turban and beard more than anything else are the outward marks of the Sikh.

Because the Sikhs regard the turban in this way they have struggled against attempts to stop them wearing it, and have seen them as acts of religious persecution. Mogul rulers failed to prevent them. In the British army Sikhs obtained the right to wear turbans instead of the steel helmet. More recently British Transport Departments have recognised the right of Sikhs to wear the turban when working on trains and buses.

Turbans are marks of responsibility and status in the East. The Mogul Emperor Akbar showed Jehangir was to be his successor by giving him 'the Turban of Empire'. Ranjit Singh gave Dosad Mohammed Khan, the Afghan ruler, a turban to mark an alliance. Turbans are given as signs of family friendship. Sikh boys in Britain often begin to wear a turban when they start school, so that they will not be ridiculed for their long hair. In India they sometimes begin to wear them when they can tie them for themselves or when they are initiated into the **Khalsa** somewhere about the age of sixteen or eighteen.

14 FESTIVALS

Sikhs have no special day in the week th[at is] regarded as a holy day for attending the **Gurdwara**. In Britain, because Sunday is a holiday, for most people this is the day they meet for worship. In the Punjab they often gather together in the evening or in the early morning.

There are a number of special anniversaries. Some are local. The martyrdom of Guru Tegh Bahadur is celebrated in Delhi, that of Guru Gobind Singh's sons at Sahind. At Chamkaur the death of Ajit Singh and Jaghar Singh, his other sons, is remembered.

The birthdays of the Gurus and especially of Nanak and Gobind Singh are celebrated universally. In 1969, at the Albert Hall in London there were special festivities for the quincentenary of Guru Nanak's birth.

A common feature of most Sikh festivals is the reading of the **Granth** from beginning to end during the forty-eight hours preceding the occasion. Often, in the cities of the Punjab, the special day is marked by a gay procession in which the **Granth** is mounted under a canopy (**palki**) on a float, a lorry or cart, and taken through the streets. Five men who represent the **panj pyare** (the original five members of the **Khalsa**), wearing yellow turbans and yellow robes with a blue sash, lead the way and are accompanied by men carrying flags with the Sikh emblem on a yellow background. Bands play while children and adults march.

There are often fairs rather like those which accompanied religious festivals in Britain in the middle ages, but the stress is often on horse-riding, wrestling and mock sword-fights.

Often many thousands of people are fed at the **guru ka langar.**

Two of the most popular Hindu festivals are **Divali** and **Holi. Divali** is the annual festival of lights in which is celebrated the victory of good over evil. It occurs in the late autumn. Sikhs celebrate it by services in the **Gurdwara** and commemorate the release of Guru Har Gobind.

Holi, occurring in early spring, is an occasion for light-hearted fun. Guru Gobind Singh replaced this with a distinctive Sikh gathering at Anandpur which almost took the form of military manoeuvres. Mock battles were staged and there were horsemanship competitions. These still survive in the celebration of **Hola Mohalla** (the Sikh name for the holiday) nowadays. The fair lasts two or three days.

Baisakhi is the most important occasion in a year free from quincentenaries and the like!

It occurs in April and marks the beginning of harvest and the hot, dry summer.

It is the beginning of New Year, the **'Bikram Year'** according to the ancient Indian lunar calendar.

Since the time of Guru Amar Das it has been one of the two occasions in the year (the other being **Divali**) when all Sikhs should assemble. Because feelings could run high on such occasions **Baisakhi** is the anniversary of a number of battles with the Moguls, and of Jallianwala Bagh in 1919.

Most important of all, however, at **Baisakhi** in 1699 Guru Gobind Singh instituted the **Khalsa** at Anandpur and it is on this day that new members are admitted into the Sikh comminity by the **Amrit** ceremony. This day is used by everyone as an opportunity for wearing new shalwar-kameeze or exchanging turbans.

Holidays for the Sikhs are still the blend of entertainment and worship that they were for Christians in medieval Europe.

15   **DEATH**   Death is the last mystery of life. It is often
accompanied by pain, if not by physical suffering at
least by the agony of leaving behind things we have
worked for and people we love. There is also the
anxiety of not knowing what lies the other side of
death. Men of many faiths believe that the present
life we are now living is only a part of the story,
that beyond death is a more wonderful life. So, as
Dietrich Bonhoeffer, the German Christian, was
going to his execution in 1945 he said, 'This is the
end: for me this is the beginning of life.' When
Louis Armstrong was a young man in New Orleans
funeral parties walked to the cemetery in tears,
lamenting the loss of a loved one, but on the way
back they danced and sang and played such music
as 'When the Saints Go Marching In' because of
their belief in the resurrection. It has been said
whosoever believes in a God must also believe in
the continuance of man after death.

To understand Sikh belief about death and life
beyond death it is necessary to glance at the Hindu
ideas from which they developed.

Hindus believe in the transmigration of the soul.
They believe that the only really important things in
the world are spirits, and that material things like
money and social position are illusions (**maya**).
We are so attached to these things that when we
die the spirit cannot gain liberation (**moksha**).
We also have to work out the results of things
we have done in our present life and eventually
become perfect. If we have been mean or quick-
tempered, in our next life we shall be placed in a
position where we shall be given opportunities to
become generous and patient. Eventually, when the
spirit has become pure, just as a precious metal or
liquid is refined or distilled, transmigration may
cease.

There are many techniques used by Hindus to

gain release. Some will go on long, exhausting dangerous pilgrimages, perhaps from the mouth of the Ganges to its source and back, others will practise asceticism, eating little and sleeping little, refusing to give in to the body. Yoga is another well-known way. The word means 'union' and the method is an attempt to liberate the spirit.

Sikhs share the Hindu belief in transmigration but believe that liberation is by the grace of God, the supreme Guru who has revealed Himself to man through the Ten Gurus.

So Guru Amar Das wrote:

'Soiled by former lives the soul is as black as jet:
Like an oily rag that could not be cleansed were
   it washed a hundred times!
But if through the Guru's grace a man dies to
   self
And be born to a new understanding,
Then the soul is free from its soiling and is not
   born again.'

When a Sikh dies the body is washed and clothed complete with all five symbols of Sikhism. It is then taken to the cremation ground in procession and hymns are sung on the way. The funeral pyre is lit by close relatives and during the cremation the **Sohila** or Bed-Time Prayer is read. One verse of it reads:

'Strive to seek that for which thou hast come
   into the world,
And through the grace of the Guru God will dwell
   in thy heart.
Thou shalt abide in His Presence, in comfort
   and peace
And not return ever
To be born and to die once more.'

When the fire has gone out and the ashes have cooled, perhaps a day or two later, they are thrown into the nearest river and the family returns home.

Either in the **Gurdwara** or in the home of the departed, relatives and friends will take part in a reading of the **Granth** at various times during the next ten days. Mourning ends with a final service when the reading has been completed.

In Britain there are no funeral pyres, but apart from taking their dead to the crematorium Sikhs attempt to follow tradition as much as possible.

F THINGS TO FIND OUT

Discover what you can about the burial customs and beliefs about life after death of Ancient Egyptians, Moslems, Jews and Christians.

The idea of rebirth is shared by all the religions which grew up in India. Try to find out more about it.

Judaism, Christianity and Islam share belief in the personal resurrection of the individual. How does this view differ from that of rebirth?

Why do some people believe that death is the end of everything?

When you have done some of the things listed above you may have enough information to be able to discuss your own ideas about life after death, either in a group or in a class debate. You might discuss the statement 'Whoever believes in a God must also believe in the continuance of man after death'.

Find out all you can about the practice of yoga in India.

16 **THE FUTURE OF SIKHS IN BRITAIN**

Many of the Asian and West Indian children now in English schools were born in Britain. They intend to stay in Britain.

Their parents may have a longing to return to their homeland, just as many Welshmen, Irishmen and Scots have; but they stay in England for the same reason as these do—and for others.

Why does an Irishman live in England? It sounds like a riddle. But the answer is not funny, even though it is simple. To work.

Wales, Scotland and Ireland cannot employ all their sons and daughters, so they come to England. Some have settled in groups in County Durham or Birmingham, and everyone knows of the 'Liverpool Irish.' Of course they are still coming, especially the Irish, to jobs which are often low paid, for example in London hotels, rather than be unemployed back home.

Work brought Asians and West Indians to Britain. It will keep them here. In their homelands they would face unemployment—as most Irish, Scots and Welsh would if they were repatriated. Even if they found work their wages would be hopelessly poor.

Other reasons keep them in Britain, especially better educational prospects for their children.

Some white Britons would like to see these immigrants repatriated; they want it to be government policy to encourage them to return home by paying their fares. Such a solution does nothing to give the immigrants work and a good standard of living when they have returned. Until opportunities in Pakistan, India and the Caribbean are as good as they are in Britain few people will return.

If they did young people would be leaving friends and their homeland to become strangers in the country of their parents!

British-born Asians would face an additional problem, the greatest stumbling block of all. Many of them do not speak Urdu or Punjabi; their native language is English.

The Sikhs are an adaptable and resilient people, otherwise they would not have survived so long. In Britain they are showing their ability to face the future in a number of ways.

Although young Sikhs are encouraged to learn Punjabi many will never understand it well enough to share in worship at the Temple. Sikh communities are aware of this and an increasing number of services are being held in English. The Sikh missionary society is publishing in English books for its children, to educate them in their faith.

Growing up in two cultures is difficult. Jews in Britain have been doing it for three or more generations; elsewhere, in Russia or India they have been living in two cultures for centuries. Understanding parents and community leaders have helped the children to find their way. Young Sikhs are being given the same assistance by their elders and there are debates within the community about the wearing of the turban, the cutting of hair, the wearing of western fashions (like the mini-skirt) by young women!

Sikh teenagers are doing much to make their communities respected in our cities. They are showing themselves to be intelligent and hard working. Knowing how their future depends upon obtaining a good education, they are striving for success in secondary schools and entering universities. At the same time, while maintaining their own values and traditions they are making lasting friendships and showing that people of different cultures can live together as one nation.

Sikhs recognise that they must fit into British society. They are adapting much more readily than most Britons who have gone abroad.

It is hoped that this book has shown that, granted this willingness to adapt where desirable, the Sikhs nevertheless cherish their freedom as we all do.

With good will and understanding the many cultures which now make up Britain should be able to live successfully together. One of the greatest signs of a mature civilisation and of a mature individual is the ability to get on with those people who hold different ideas and traditions, and to respect their views and beliefs.

At Southall in Middlesex, the Sikh Foundation has now opened a Punjabi School to prepare boys and girls for G.C.E. O-level examinations in Punjabi and to give instructions in the Sikh faith. This is one way in which the community is helping the young generation to maintain its Sikh culture and identity.

Part of the opening ceremony, the Punjabi School, Southall.

FUTURE OF SIKHS IN BRITAIN

INFORMATION FOR TEACHERS

There are not many books about the Sikhs
available in England.
A few are:
> **Sikhism** W. O. Cole and P. S. Sambhi *Ward Lock*
> **A History of the Sikhs** (2 vols.) Khushwant
> Singh *Oxford University Press*
> **Guru Nanak and the Sikh Religion**
> W. H. McLeod *Oxford University Press*
> **The Sacred Writings of the Sikhs** *Allen*
> *and Unwin*

Pamphlets and collections of stories and much
helpful information can be obtained from:

Mrs. Pamela Wylam, 17, Abbotshall Rd,
London SE6 1SQ
The Sikh Cultural Society, 88, Mollison Way,
Edgware, Mddx.
The Sikh Missionary Society (U.K.), 27 Pier
Road, Gravesend.

Annually a list of aids to the teachings of the
religions of the world is produced by the Shap
Working Party on World Religions in Education
and the Divinity Department of Borough Road
College of Education. These can be obtained
from: The Divinity Department (W.R.), Borough
Road College, Isleworth, Mddx.
Educational Productions have recently
produced a filmstrip portraying Sikhism in India,
also one showing the *Amrit* initiation rite. **The
Sikh Religion** (Concordia) describes the Sikh
life and worship in Britain.
Immigration and Integration Clifford Hill,
Pergamon, and **Colour and Citizenship,**
E. J. B. Rose and Associates, *Oxford University
Press*, contain important references to the Sikh
community in Britain.

CONVERSION TABLE

The Republic of India uses the metric system for all measurements. The rupee, not the pound sterling, is the unit of currency.

If you obtain fact sheets from the High Commission of India or the Commonwealth Institute, or if you read books which have been published in India you may find the following information useful.

Length	0.914 metre	= 1 yard
	1.609 kilometres	= 1 mile
	8 kilometres	= 5 miles (approximately)
Area	1 are	= 1 hectare
	259 hectares	= 1 square mile
	(640 acres	= 1 square mile)
	1 hectare	= $2\frac{1}{2}$ acres (approximately)
Capacity	28.317 cubic metres	= 1000 cubic feet
Weight	1 kilogram	= 2.2 lbs.
	1,016 kilograms	= 1 ton

Temperature. To change centigrade to fahrenheit multiply by 9/5 and add 32 degrees.

Money. 18 rupees (written Rs 18) = £1 sterling, that is 100 new pence. A rupee is divided into 100 **paises**.

N.B. The Pakistan rupee has a rate of 25.55 to 100 new pence (it is divided into 100 **paises**)

Other terms you may come across:

1 tonne	= 1000 kilograms	
1 lakh (lac)	= 100,000	these are shorthand ways
1 crore	= 10 million	of writing large numbers.

GLOSSARY

Glossary of terms found in this book or which may be encountered in further reading. Page references indicate the main source of information if the word is used in this book.

Adi	first
Amrit	nectar of immortality. Initiation ceremony (pp. 51–2, 71–2)
Amritsar	city of Nectar. Holy City of the Sikhs. (p. 41)
Baba	'father'. A term of respect applied to Hindu, Moslem or Sikh men of piety.
Baisakhi	Indian lunar month. Sikh and Buddhist festival. According to many traditions the month in which Nanak was born. (p. 92)
Bhai	brother—applied to Sikhs of learning and piety.
Chela	disciple.
Chapatti	unleavened, flat-baked, wholemeal bread.
Dasam	tenth.
Diwali, Divali or Dipavali	Indian festival of Lights, Lakshmi festival, harvest, occurring in October/November.
Diwan	Court of an Indian prince. Sikh assembly for worship.
doab	land between two rivers.
dupatta	muslim scarf worn by a Sikh woman over her head and shoulders. (p. 89)
faqir	Moslem ascetic.
ghat	bathing-place or place where corpses are cremated.
Granth	the book containing the Sikh scriptures.
gurdwara	Sikh Temple.
guru	spiritual teacher, sometimes the divine inner voice.
guru bani or gurbani	the voice of the guru, the hymns of the Granth.
halal meat	meat from an animal slaughtered according to Moslem custom (p. 74)
harmandar	the house of the Lord, the Golden Temple at Amritsar.
janam sakhi	tradition biography.
japji	the principal Sikh meditation composed by Guru Nanak for morning prayer (pp. 35, 52).
kameeze	dress (part of 'trouser suit' worn by Sikh women). (p. 89)
kachs	shorts (p. 53)
kanga	comb. (p. 53)
kara	steel bracelet. (p. 53)
karah parshad	communion food of the Sikhs (p. 67)
kesh	long hair. (p. 53)
khalsa	the Sikh brotherhood instituted by Guru Gobind Singh. (p. 51)
kirpan	sword. (p. 53)
langar	(guru ka langar—temple of bread) free kitchen. (p. 40)
Nam	the divine name. (p. 37)
palki	palanquin, upon which the Granth is placed.
pir	a Moslem saint, a sufi.
sangat	/organisation of Sikhs.
sati Nam	the True Name, a Sikh way of referring to God.
Shalwar	long trousers worn by Sikh women. (p. 89)
Sufi	Moslem mystic.
Takht	throne upon which the Granth is placed.
Waheguru	wonderful Lord, used to describe God.